30
3
2p

Assistants.

LETTERS

FROM

A MOURNING CITY

(NAPLES. AUTUMN, 1884)

BY

AXEL MUNTHE

TRANSLATED FROM THE SWEDISH BY
MAUDE VALÉRIE WHITE

LONDON

JOHN MURRAY, ALBEMARLE STREET

1887

Pte Jas Wilson
No 632 ? B Coy.
1st Batt Cam Hdrs
Inverness

Printed by R. & R. CLARK, *Edinburgh.*

PREFACE

HESE letters date from a little trip
to Naples during the autumn of
1884. They were written by a
tourist who had given himself a
holiday, and who had made straight for the
place to which he felt himself most attracted.
The people amongst whom he moved were
hampered by no sort of authority, no more
was he; no sort of tie bound him to any
sort of recognised organisation whatsoever. He
went where he pleased as in former days. He
is an old traveller, and like most people who
have been a good deal abroad, has given up
writing his name in the Visitors' Book. Unknown he arrived, and unknown, thank God,
he took himself off.

These letters, which first appeared in the

Stockholm *Dagblad*, were written under circumstances scarcely favourable to literary pursuits, and in a frame of mind not calculated to inspire polished phrases and well-turned figures of speech,—they were written *sur pied de guerre*. It was only after considerable hesitation that the author consented to their publication in book form, and then his first idea was to work them out, correct their numerous deficiencies, and suppress whatever struck him as unsatisfactory. That plan, however, he was obliged to abandon, for he soon discovered that were he to carry it out, very few of them would survive the operation. He then made up his mind to let them be, leaving the task of suppression to the critic. Something might be allowed to stand over, he hoped, his affectionate gratitude to Italy if nothing else.

And let it be remembered that he rode a broken-winded little donkey, no strong-winged Pegasus—do not forget that the donkey was so tiny that he could not prevent his legs from dragging along the ground.

Besides which, Rosina is old and failing; it will not do to be too hard upon her, if only for the sake of leaving her undisturbed in the philosophical researches which she still con-

tinues to pursue. He has no such eloquent
reasons to urge on his behalf; but before the
critics make up their minds to eat him up alive,
let them look out, for it is just possible that
they might swallow a few cholera microbes into
the bargain. . . .

PARIS, *December* 1886.

I

ARTENZA per Napoli !" So
rang the cry through the railway station in Rome.

We were a crowd of travellers gathered
together in the refreshment room, all busy
eating; I was tired and hungry after my
long journey, and had just retired into
a corner where I was utilising the few
remaining moments in hastily swallowing
my Roman luncheon.   The man who
had announced the train looked in at the
door, but no one stirred from their seat;
he then came up to the table at which I
was sitting, and all the occupants of the
dining-room dropped their knives and
forks in utter astonishment, eyeing me

B

with considerable curiosity as he said to me : " *Lei va a Napoli, è vero ?* "

Yes, I certainly was going to Naples, and hurried off immediately to secure a good place ; an unnecessary precaution, for when the train started I was alone in the *coupé*, at Marino I discovered that I was alone in the carriage, and at Albano it became quite evident that I was the only passenger in the train.

An appalling stench of carbolic acid filled the carriages.

Never before had I travelled at such a pace in Italy. The train rushed madly over Velletri, Segni, Anagni, Ferentino—all old acquaintances of former travelling days— and before I knew where I was, we had reached Ceprano, where there was a delay of five minutes, as I found out from the guard, who was bestowing all his attention on me, seeing that there was no other hope of a *pourboire* in the train. Ceprano is the usual resting-place between Rome and Naples ; I just happened to remember.

that a particularly good old wine was obtainable in this part of the world, and ran hastily into the refreshment room ; but it was empty, and an old woman who sat outside spinning, informed me that nothing was to be had there : "*Non vengono più nessuni,*" said she sadly.

On we sped over Liris, the beautiful river with the beautiful name, and to the left, high up on the mountain, lay the gray old convent of Monte Casino, greeting me with peaceful recollections of bygone times, of quiet working-days spent amongst the convent archives, where I had turned over many a monk-written chronicle and dreamed thoughts, how different to the actual thoughts of the present day. . . .

And the train rushed noisily on over Teano, Sparanisi, Pignataro, over the valley of Volturno, gradually approaching the land of summer. Before us lay the Terra di Lavoro in all the splendour of its gorgeous colouring, the green elm-trees and fragrant roses had quite forgotten that summer was over, but the vines were glowing in all their rich autumnal beauty, and heavy clusters of ripe grapes were waiting to yield their young wine.

It was just beginning to grow dusky, and I suppose I must have fallen asleep for a minute or so; I recollect being under the impression that the smell of carbolic acid was increasing every moment, and was gradually spreading through the open windows all down the road along which we were travelling. An icy draught, as though some one had opened the door, blew over me, extinguishing the lamp that hung from the ceiling; I shivered suddenly, an irresistible inexplicable feeling that I was no longer alone, shot through me, and I felt the cold perspiration on my forehead. And at the same time it seemed to me that the carriage had turned into a coffin, flying rapidly over the dusky plains, and that Death and I were alone together, and beneath my closed eyelids I felt my gloomy fellow-traveller gazing fixedly at me from the corner opposite. . . .

Slight carbolic acid poisoning + sleepless night + considerable nervous excitement, eh, doctor? But anyhow the lamp was out.

At Capua a man really did turn up who was going on by the same train; he came to the door of my carriage, and, contrary to my usual habits, I felt quite sociably inclined. He had a head like Augustus, and the proud mouth relaxed into a derisive smile at the strong smell of carbolic acid that met him as he opened the door. I felt ashamed of my funereal meditations, and thought to myself: here at any rate is a fellow who does not know what fear is. Such at least was the impression he gave me; he glanced at me that very moment, as though he had been able to read my thoughts—for an instant only, but very contemptuously, it seemed to me.

We made no attempt at conversation, both of us were on our dignity, he reserved as a Cæsar, I morose as a plebeian. The train had now reached Caserta ; desolate and deserted as all the other wayside stations. Suddenly the door of the carriage next to ours was thrown open, and two guards ran hastily towards the station-house, carrying between them the conductor of the train who had been in to look at our tickets only an hour ago ; the light of the lantern fell upon the waxen face, which I hardly recognised, so great was the terror that shone out of his wide open eyes. The supercilious stranger and myself glanced involuntarily at each other, and the same words fell simultaneously from our lips—*il cholera !* And I took back all I had thought to myself when he had first come up to the carriage sneering at the strong smell of carbolic acid, for the brave fellow grew paler and paler, retiring into the furthermost corner of the carriage, and binding his pocket-handkerchief tightly round his nose and mouth. Presently the other conductor returned, and

I noticed, as he wiped the perspiration off his brow, that, half surreptitiously, he made the sign of the cross with his hand ; I beckoned to him to come up to our carriage, and he then told me that the poor man was the second conductor who had sickened in the train during the last fortnight ; he thought his companion would be better here in Caserta than in Naples, where the hospitals were already overcrowded.

Naturally, since my companion had wrapped his mouth up in his pocket-handkerchief, there was less likelihood than ever of our engaging in conversation, and he looked angrily and suspiciously at me into the bargain, especially after my little chat through the window with the guard. He got out at Cancello, and the new conductor—who was now looking after me with an amount of attention which was in inverse proportion to the distance from Naples, where the *pourboire* was to make its appearance—informed me that he

believed it was *il sindaco*, the mayor of
Cancello himself, whom we had had with
us. It is in Cancello that the upward
mails from Naples are delayed for a whole
day to be disinfected—saturated with
sulphur, sprinkled with carbolic acid, etc.
I remember wondering how far *il sindaco* superintended this ceremony himself, and what he would look like during
the process. But it isn't fair to be
hard upon him, especially if he be no
exception to the rule that fear paves the
way for cholera, for in that case he may
be lying ill at this very moment—he
often came into my mind when reading
over the provincial bulletins.

And as I sat alone in the half-dark
railway carriage, bright memories of former
days began to light up the road along
which we were travelling. It was again
over Campagna Felice, over "the happy
fields" that the September moon was
just rising ; it was "Italy's paradise," and
all the joys of my youth that were again

stretching out their arms to me, and
"*Napoli la bella*" that was, as of old, bidding me welcome to the sound of song
and guitar! Across the bay flew soft
breezes with greetings from Sorrento, and
far away, like the most beautiful *fata morgana* on earth, lay the blue island of
Capri floating in the distance. And the
repulsive smell of carbolic acid inside the
carriage oppressed me no longer, the
withered roses of past summers filled the
air again with all their fragrance, and
kindly thoughts of heartfelt gratitude to
the lovely country that lay before me,
awoke from out their winter's sleep, wherein they had lain through many a busy
working-day, far off from sun and summer.

Never before had I known the strength
of the link which bound me to this country
—it is not in the bright moments of life
that we realise how deeply we cherish a
friend, it is when we know him to be
unhappy and in distress, that the hidden
voices of our inmost hearts break forth

into their own language, which knows not
how to lie, and give utterance to the soul's
most silent thoughts. Naples lies mourning now, shall we not all hasten thither,
even as unto a fellow-creature in distress,
we who have spent such happy days in
her midst, we who have learnt to love her
simple, warm - hearted, poverty - stricken
children ; we who have heard the mando-
line sound across the bay to the strains
of *"O dolce Napoli !"* we who from Camaldoli's convent heights have beheld the
loveliest vision that ever greeted the eye
of man, when the sun goes down behind the
Ischian hills, and when the roseate light,
which no brush can paint, floods the
mountains of Sorrento, when Capri spreads
her veil of ever-increasing blue across her
own fair island, and over the green-coloured
velvet slopes of Vesuvius, fall the tints of
that deep violet that can never be forgotten ! Dost thou remember the nightingale's song in the groves about Sorrento,
when the orange-trees were in full bloom,

when thou satest listening all through the soft, still summer's night to the dreamy songs from some poor fisherman's boat far out on the bay, and fellest asleep to the last sounds of *"Felicissima notte! addio, addio!"* still ringing in thine ears, like unto a lingering farewell to the happiest days of thy life?

And now is the time to give back to Italy a tithe of all she has given us! Here is room for every one, poor and rich can be of equal use, here where the distress is so great and declares itself in so many ways; here strong arms are needed to bear the sick, here strong heads are needed to think over and carry out the plans for allaying the misery that is stalking through the land. You need bring nothing with you but pity for a suffering so great that it has no name, and if the love you bore to Italy still lives within you, so much the greater will your patience be, so much the softer the hands that shall nurse the poor sufferers! And if it should cost you your life, well, what of that! Is it then so sweet to live, and is it so hard to die, when one can die in the land of one's dreams, knowing that one has helped others to live, or if their fate is sealed, that one has at least helped them to die! Ye who are rich, give, give of your abundance, here are a thousand mouths crying for bread ; and ye who are poor, light ye in kindly thought a votive candle on the altar of your silent intercessions.

Pure nervousness + innate sentimentality + blind love towards Italy + suspicious tendency to mysticism—is the fellow a Catholic? eh, doctor?

The train glided into the Naples station. The platform was empty, not a single gesticulating *facchino* ready to tear the things out of your hands, not a single one of the drivers outside, standing up on the box of their own cabs, cracking their whips and crying, "*Ecco Signori, buona carozzella, buonissimo cavallo!*" no deafening welcome from the street life of Naples, in the shape of the hundred urchins who swarm round every newcomer, swinging their arms one moment, standing on their heads the next, with outstretched hands, crying, " *Date u soldo, eccellenza, u bajocco, Signorì !* " And my friend Pasqualino, who was all-in-all to me last time I was here, why has he not come down to carry my luggage home for me ? yet I had certainly written to his mother, my old padrona, asking her to prepare my former room for me. What has become of every one ? A dark and ominous silence has fallen over all the streets, and it begins to dawn upon me why my poor Pasqualino has not come down to meet the train.

Here we are at my old lodgings, over the doorway I read the following words, " Closed on account of cholera-infection " —Pasqualino was dead, my dear old landlady was dead, her black-eyed little Teresina was dead !

II

IT is in times like these, in the midst of cholera and unequalled poverty, that the popular character is brought to light and exposed in all its weakness, but also in all its beauty. No doubt help has come from every part of the country, from every part of the world; but even here, as is so often the case, it is the poor who have exercised the greatest charity, the silent self-sacrificing devotion has come from those who have next to nothing themselves. Who has given most, the wealthy banker who is publicly thanked for having presented the town with 1000 francs, or the poor contadino who comes up to the hospital dragging his only goat along with him, though he had meant to keep it for Christmas, and the Mergellina fisherman, who, after a whole night out at sea, silently empties the contents of his net upon the threshold of his sick neighbour's door— have you the heart to laugh because he has reserved a few fish and sold them under way, in order to buy the candle which is burning now beneath the Blessed Virgin's picture in the sickroom !

All the praise falls to the share of those aristocrats who have presented the Relief Committee with so many pairs of sheets and shirts, their names have figured in all the newspapers, but have they all together given as much as the obscure young fishwife of Vico Grotta Santa whom I saw last night ? The story is not long, would you like to hear it ?

Anarella—for such is her name—had already attracted my attention yesterday, when I was up in the little lane in which she lives ; she had even then taken my

part in a discussion that had arisen between some of her neighbours and myself.
A fisherman, who shared her husband's
boat, had been struck down with cholera
the day before, and had been removed by
one of the ambulance societies, almost by
force, to the hospital, where I accidentally
came across him.   He was still conscious,
but utterly exhausted ; he cried continually
for his wife and child, and as it was out of
my power to do anything for the man
himself, I promised him that I would at
least go and look after them.   He died
shortly afterwards.   By the time I reached
his home, both wife and child had been
attacked, and the wife died towards evening.   She must have been a general
favourite amongst her neighbours, as far
as I was able to judge by the poignancy
of their grief and the loudness of their
lamentations, and I heard a low mur-
mur of "*avvelenatore*," "*assassino*," etc.,[1] run
through the crowd below.   And I found

[1] Poisoner, murderer.

it singularly difficult to convince them that if I had not been able to save her, I was at least innocent of her death — her husband's death they had expected from the moment he had been taken to the hospital, from whence, according to the popular belief, no one ever returns.

It was then that Anarella undertook to plead my cause, which consisted chiefly in the assurance that she herself had seen me taste the medicine before giving it to the sick woman—this appears to have considerably raised my value in the market, and I was left in peace.

Meanwhile the house had become infected from top to bottom, and two fresh cases of cholera occurred that night. As I happened to be on the spot, I glanced round the room in which the mother's corpse still lay. Some lighted candles had been placed by the bed, and beside her lay the child on a heap of rags inside a fishing-basket—it was still alive, but

C

vavama,[1] who was sitting there thumbing her rosary, knew as well as I did that it was dying, whether of starvation or cholera, it was difficult to say.   I sent the old woman off to try and get some milk, but she came back, having been unable to procure any.   Whilst I was endeavouring to convey to the old grandmother how more and more decidedly I inclined to the double diagnosis of cholera and starvation, —the poor old thing looked as though she had had plenty of personal experience of what the latter meant,—Anarella came into the room.   She looked at the child for a moment, saying in an undertone, "*Poverina ! poverina !*"[2] then took it out of the basket, and with a superb gesture, which I shall never forget, she tore open her ragged old fishing jacket and put the child to her breast.

At that very moment her husband entered the room ; he has been a pilot,

---

[1] Neapolitan dialect, *la mia nonna*—grandmother.

[2] Poor little one.

and there isn't much that he is afraid of, still he shared the people's unutterable dread of cholera, and had come to take his wife away from the infected house. When he saw her with the babe at her breast he grew pale ; he knew that it was at the risk, not only of her own life, but at that of their own healthy child's, but he said nothing, and only crossed himself in silence. And if I remember rightly, the doctor did the same himself.

*　　*

*

Ah yes, it is quite true that the popular character is brought to light and exposed in all its weakness in times like these. But one friendly effort to look upon life from these poor people's point of view, will help you to understand and patiently excuse, many things which would jar upon you otherwise, and teach you at all events to care for this crassly ignorant, but warm - hearted and long - suffering people. And then will the aristocrat's white hand no longer shun the lazzarone's rags, then will the philosopher no longer find it in his heart to raise a laugh at the people's blind superstitions concerning the Madonna and San Gennaro (the patron saint of Naples), then will the doctor refuse the revolver which he has been advised to carry, in order to shield himself from the outbreaks of popular fanaticism during his night rounds in the poor quarter. (The complaints that have been so often raised of late are, alas, only too well founded : doctors have been attacked over and over again by the sick people's relations, and have repeatedly been obliged to defend their own lives.) But I don't think the danger is so very great after all ; a little patient sympathy with the sick, a little bread to the hungry crowd around, and a little forbearance towards their attitude of defiant suspicion, is more effective than a pistol shot or an escort of two carabiniers with their clanking swords at your heels.

And a doctor must not be too particular with regard to the consideration in which his profession is held, nor must he be too sensitive as to the amount of faith which the poor people repose in his skill ; the lazzaroni are as sceptical with regard to the infallibility of his medicines as the doctor very likely is himself in the inmost depths of his heart. But they go a step further, and are of opinion that all sorts of horrors lie at the bottom of their mixtures—various poisons " the evil eye," serpents' tongues, a few hairs off the devil's head, etc. etc., ingredients which, to the best of my belief, are not usually included in the pharmacopœia. The patient himself is as a rule too ill to offer much resistance, but those who stand around follow every movement of the doctor's with the profoundest suspicion. I knew a doctor who, every time he endeavoured to dose a patient, was greeted with these

words, "*Bevete voi primo*," [1] and of course
he did so—the only objection to this mutual
drug-drinking (which may perhaps be
recommended to certain mixture-loving
physicians) being that the doctor, who is
not down with cholera, is pretty sure to feel
rather sleepy after all the opium drops. . . .

This introduction to doctors and
officials is, after all, so new an experience
for the inhabitants of the poor quarters,
that one can almost understand their
mistrust.   At ordinary times no policeman
goes near the place—which no doubt
tends to impart a certain comfortable
sensation to many a black-eyed fellow,
whose conscience, may be, is no cleaner
than his face.   And the inhabitants of the
fondaci, *bassi*, and *sottoterrani* of the
Mercato, Pendino, Porto, and Vicaria
quarters, come into the world and go
out of it without the doctor's assistance
in either one case—or the other.   But
often enough through the little aperture,

[1] Taste it first yourself.

which in these sort of houses serves the purpose of both window and door, a lean old monk may be seen slipping in. . . .

A propos of monks, as we have perhaps had enough cholera for to-day, let me wind up my letter by devoting a few words to them !

The critic shakes his head as he reads the following words in the above paragraph, " a *lean* old monk ;" there isn't a novel or a book of travels on Italy in which monks are not invariably represented as red-cheeked and corpulent, and our Italian authorities and æsthetic oracles at home — especially if they happen to be fat themselves — refuse point-blank to allow the monks to grow thin ; but the poor old fellows have done so all the same, since they have been harried to death by United Italy, and I beg to enter a protest against these gentlemen's classical representation of the typical fat monk. I know that it is part and parcel of a modern description of Italy to have a hit at the monks.   Every traveller itching to reduce his impressions to black and white (scribbling and malaria are the two diseases which invariably attack travellers in this part of the world, more especially Northerners, and they are both equally disagreeable to come across), though he may know no more about Italy than what he has read in Bædaeker's handbook, though he may never have felt the heart of Italy's ideal beauty beating beneath the bark, is at all events able to report on the number of round-faced monks whom he has seen tossing off their bumpers and gormandising *ad libitum*. I am well aware that it isn't popular to stand up for the monks, but I mean to do so all the same—and indeed it is no more than my bounden duty, for I number many a good friend amongst the kindly old brothers.   As it is, they have such a wretched time of it, these poor remaining monks, they are so timid in the consciousness that wherever they go they must silently and uncomplainingly accept the scorn and raillery which is their daily bread ; perhaps it is on that account that they get on best with the poor, who always treat them kindly.

Poor old monks ! they are doomed to extinction in any case,—why not let them depart in peace?

And they are not my only *protégés*. I have others besides them, and now that we are on the subject I may as well produce them from the hidden depths of my compassionate sympathy. Were I ruler over a vast, vast kingdom, I would divide the lands into three equal parts, and deal it out to the three innocent victims of modern civilisation : monks, Laplanders, and Red Indians. But how would they all get on together—that is the question ? I wonder whether the Redskins would modify their bad habits to the extent of scalping one another only, or whether, when their old inclinations were roused, they would try their hand on my other subjects as well ? But I should wander about my kingdom and try to keep things straight, and of one thing I am quite sure, I should be on good terms with the whole lot !—Or perhaps, all things taken into consideration, I might abdicate and turn monk myself. . . .

III

AFTER having raged for a whole month with fearful rapidity, the cholera began to diminish, and the poor sorrow-stricken town of Naples to hope that her days of mourning were over. The voluntary ambulances granted a sorely-needed holiday to part of their staff, the great fires that had been lit at night in all the squares were discontinued, the strong smell of sulphur that had filled the air for so long, diminished gradually, the shops in the Strada di Toledo took down their shutters one after the other, there was traffic in the streets again, and the mayor telegraphed to the king that the epidemic had come to an end.

And the fruiterers began to smuggle in fresh figs from Sorrento, the beautiful blue luscious figs, of which the sale had been forbidden since the outbreak of the cholera ; and the little osterias, " *bettole*," which had been closed for more than three weeks, began to lure in, one after the other, the thirsty customers unable any longer to resist the temptation of drowning the recollection of so many anxious days and nights in a glass of *vino nuovo*.

Now October was just at hand, when it was the people's custom to celebrate their merriest holidays in the *osterias* of Posilipo, in order to taste the first wine of the year, which had just been got ready about that time, Gragnano, Vino del Monte, del Vesuvio, del Procida, and whatever they are all called ; and last Thursday, on the *Ottobrata* holiday, the sound of guitars and mandolines was heard in Posilipo as of old, and the tarantella's strains awoke the slumbering gladness to new life again —*E morto il cholera, evviva la gioia !*

Naples heaved a deep sigh of relief
after her long spell of anguish, every one
was in good spirits and on friendly terms,
and every one felt as if they must congratulate each other upon the gloomy
days that were over at last. *Whom* to
thank for the fortunate and unexpected
turn that things had taken, they hardly
knew themselves ; every one had something
to say on the subject, and the newspapers
rang the praises of first one and then the
other. The official authorities thanked
the king, whose courage and energy had
put new life into every one, the middle
classes thanked the Municipality and the
Relief Committees, and the people, the
poor people who had suffered most—they
thanked the Mother of God. And I
think the people were right. They had
lit votive candles at her shrines when the
distress was at its height ; when death
had entered almost all their homes, they
had implored her assistance, and now
that deliverance seemed at hand, humble

and grateful they kissed the hem of her garment.

The present generation, grown old enough to have outgrown its faith in God, laughs at all this "superstition"; but I am one with the lazzaroni on that score ; it is certainly very easy to live without God Almighty in prosperity and health, but I am beginning to realise that it is a good deal harder to die without Him.

I wish I had a collection of new-fledged young atheists out here, and that I were able to take them with me through the poor quarters of the town, where sorrow and misery are at home. I would show them the peace which the consolations of religion are able to bring to the closing eyes of even these poor creatures, who might certainly be excused for thinking that their debt of gratitude to God Almighty is no large one ; I would show them that the crucifix over the bed is better able to soothe the pangs of death than all the doctors' morphine syringes.

Ah, "there is more in heaven and earth than our philosophy has dreamt of"—and our science too for the matter of that; and perhaps such a sight as this might shake their reasoned philosophies, no matter from what source of wisdom they had been drawn, and precipitate the pure gold of their childhood's simple faith to the bottom of their souls.

But still, even though philosophy were silenced, we have the profound researches of science to fall back upon, the magnificent triumphs of medicine, and its brilliant discoveries! Well and good! amidst the *olla-podrida* of dead theories and living microbes, of groping experiments and troubled mixtures—"*la main sur la conscience*," what poor insignificant charlatans are not we all the same, and how little able to compete with the the other Physician whose practice is so large, and who goes about from bed to bed with his one and only drug, his eternal sleeping draught!

The poor ignorant people here knew at least to whom to carry their troubles and anxieties ; they had from the first confided all their sorrows to the Mother of God. When every one else had abandoned them, her arms had always been stretched out to them ; no matter how ragged they might be, she knew how to help them all.

And those who sneered at their superstitions and forbad their processions, what had they to offer them in exchange for their obscure but rock-like faith? Ah yes, sanitary rules, veritable sarcasms on their poverty, printed advertisements, which most of them were unable to read and none of them were able to understand, recommending them to live in airy rooms, to avoid vegetables, and take to meat, to disinfect constantly, either with carbolic acid, which is an excellent remedy according to one Sanitary Committee, but no good according to another, or with " corrosive sublimate," the most effective microbe antidote according to Dr. Koch—

although the idea that it is useless is quite worthy of consideration also.

And what has the obtuse brain of a lazzarone to do with Koch and microbes, he whose thoughts have never crossed the bay beyond which the whole of the remaining world is " Barbaria " to him, he who knows a host of saints' days, a few prayers that he has been taught as a child, the names of a dozen fish he has seen jumping in the nets at Mergellina, he who can play at *morra* and sing *Santa Lucia*, and that is about all ! How is he to manage to " air the room," he who lives with ten or twelve others in one of those *fondaci*, into which the light of day has never been known to penetrate, where one of us is unable to remain for more than a moment without going out to take a breath of fresh air ! And he is, forsooth, to choose his food, he whose expenses at the best of times never exceed one or two soldi a day, he who never in his life has had the chance of

D

tasting meat, and whom you may perhaps see standing in front of the baker's shop, watching, with the expression of a hungry animal in his eyes, the piece of bread which you have just given your dog, and then fighting over the remaining crumbs with a crowd of others such as himself!——

And as to disinfection! what does he know about that, he who, alas, shows so little inclination to master the first great rule of disinfection, the popular antiseptic which consists in sometimes dipping one's hands and face in water. . . .

Just give a thought to all this, and then it will no longer strike you as so wonderful that these poor people should believe more in the censer's clouds than in the sulphur's fumes, and more in holy water than in a ten per cent solution of carbolic acid.

*   *

*

I had lingered in Posilipo last Thursday evening, and it was already late as I sauntered home towards the town. In the Strada di Piedegrotta sat a boy singing *La bella Sorrentina*—

"Io te vidi a Piedegrotta
Tutta gioia, tutta festa."

And a little further on I halted for a moment at Mergellina to let the sea-breeze blow over me, whilst I watched the fishing-smacks as one by one they sailed home from their day's work out on the bay. From Villa Reale there were sounds of music and dancing, and the Chiaia was swarming with people as though it were a feast-day ; and it was a feast-day in deed and truth, the cholera had ceased, and it was the first day of that year on which they had been allowed to taste the new wine! *E morto il cholera, evviva la gioia!*

But no—it was not dead. During the night the grim guest had gone his rounds again, and when Naples awoke next morning, several fresh cases of cholera were reported to have occurred the previous day, and the authorities were unable

to conceal the fact that the epidemic had
broken out again with renewed virulence.
I see no reason for transcribing the official
bulletins published in the newspapers ;
they have already been transmitted by
telegraph, and their numbers have no
other significance than that of announcing
the increase or decrease of the epidemic.
That the figures have always been kept
too low is a well-known fact here, and no
one has ever made a secret of it.   That
the figures of the dead are as untrust-
worthy as those of the sick, I was able to
see for myself yesterday evening, when I
was up at the cholera cemetery ; I must
have remained there a good hour, and
during that time alone, eighty-three bodies
were left there (the official report of the
day announcing fifty-seven deaths and no
more).

The dead are laid in a row before
they are buried.   We bent over every
one of them ; it was impossible to make
any mistake : they had all died that

day. After they have been lowered into
the grave, their names are written down
in the register. The impression produced
by the quantity of blank spaces in the
book is singularly uncanny, nothing but
a number to distinguish them, anonymous dead, homeless during their lifetime,
one common cholera grave after their
death !

Several hundred of these nameless dead
lie sleeping there since the outbreak of
the epidemic ; ah yes ! they also had a
name of their own, which was about all
that society had ever bestowed on them—
but Death has grudged them even that.
They certainly had a name of their own,
which once upon a time was whispered
lovingly over them in the most melodious
language on earth, when they were infants
sleeping on their mother's knee ; but perhaps the only one who knew it had pre-
ceded them to the grave, or perhaps the
hungry little orphans who at this very
moment are wandering about the filthy

alleys of the poor quarter are the only ones who might be able to tell us something about them——no one knows anything about them up here, a number round each one's neck in turn, no coffin, no shroud, nothing but a covering of quicklime.   And so on to the next one.

IV

HE unexpected reappearance
of the cholera last week led to a
fearful panic. In a single day
the town became as empty and as silent
as during the worst days of the epidemic ;
the streets again reeked of the horrid
smell of sulphur, and through the night
the fires burned as before in the public
squares ; the ambulance societies, which
had begun to disperse, again prepared
themselves for instant action, and to all
appearance the days of mourning were
about to recommence for the poor town
of Naples. The people began to lose
their power of endurance, and a certain
agitation of evil omen was noticeable in

the poor quarters. The municipal authorities did their best to compose the minds of the multitude, and the newspapers were again recommended to dissemble the real state of affairs. Doctors here have been speculating upon the reasons of this violent and unforeseen increase of cases, and the newspapers are still full of such discussion. Most of them have come to the conclusion that the real cause is to be traced to *il vino nuovo*, which was tried rather too often on the Ottobrata feast-day, last Thursday. As one proof of how the day was abused, a correspondent quotes a merry party of four lazzaroni who suddenly discovered themselves to be rich enough to buy twenty-four litres of *vino di Posilipo*, and who, bewildered perhaps at the novelty of the situation, and determined to wipe out every trace thereof—tossed off the whole lot there and then. The gay party wound up at the Conocchia hospital, every one of them being struck down with cholera during the night.

The idea that the recrudescence of the epidemic is due to the excesses of Thursday's holiday is of course a reassuring, but not, I am afraid, a correct one. I cannot understand how doctors can bring themselves to believe that one day's wine-drinking is sufficient to account for so sudden an increase of cases ; that amongst the joyous crowd who up at Posilipo on Thursday last drank a farewell toast to the cholera, many were subsequently attacked, I am quite willing to believe ; but allowing the minimum of time for the incubation of cholera, it is nevertheless longer than the hours which transpired between Thursday evening and Friday morning, when most of the cases were announced. Without wishing to enter into this question, which is out of place here, my own opinion is that the increase of the epidemic may be traced to the varied temperature of the last few days, (a sudden fall of the barometer, a change of wind, condition of the water underground, etc.) A careful observation of the patients at the hospital—who had certainly nothing to do with Thursday's merry-makings—inclines me to this view, for the greater part of them exhibited a considerable change for the worse, coinciding exactly in point of time with the outbreak in the town.

Besides, and this is an experience corroborated by most people here, any sudden change of temperature must interfere with the process of digestion, and must for that very reason predispose reception of disease. Another fact not willingly admitted but nevertheless indubitable—a certain laxity has crept into the Sanitary Society's administrations, extending even to the doctors themselves. As far as these latter are concerned it is not to be wondered at—human beings, like the rest of us, physical exhaustion is bound to assert itself sooner or later, and they have had a hard time of it. For the first weeks everything went without a hitch,

most of them (and to the honour of the
medical staff of Naples be it said) went
to their duty through fire, risking their
own lives to save the lives of others.
To the sense of duty that bade them
stand at their post must be added the
scientific interest, which was the magnet
that attracted a goodly number; here
were many experiences to be gained,
many dark riddles to be solved—many
laurels to be won.   It is as yet too early
in the day to decide how far Science has
been satisfied, but this much I can tell
you : if, as we are given to understand,
the deepest interest centres in the *search*
after Truth, then the doctors have every
reason to congratulate themselves, and
their zeal ought to be more ardent than
ever—for nothing has been discovered.
They have gone forward to meet this
epidemic with fresh weapons, with all
the most important results of recent experiences, Koch's discovery of the cholera
microbes, etc. etc., but one can only bear

witness to the fact how much yet remains
to be discovered, ere we can hope to attain
to some positive practical result as to the
special *treatment* which the cholera patient
requires,—if such a result be indeed attain-
able at all.

And this outbreak has been if anything
more terrible than the last ; 10,000 cases
taken *en bloc* give a mortality of 6000 ;
and in certain infected quarters the mortality has increased to eighty per cent (at
Fuorigrotto, in the neighbourhood of
Naples, twenty-five out of twenty-nine
patients died ; the death-rate of Torre
del Greco and several other suburbs has
been enormous).   If the hygienic and
therapeutic conditions of the town are not
all that they might be, the hospitals,
on the other hand, have been well served
by able men, and eager investigators.
Everything has been tried, very little
headway made.   I, who have casually
been brought into contact with some
hundred cholera patients, have arrived

at a very profound conclusion with which I am quite willing to acquaint you here, where there is no chance of the doctors overhearing us. To my mind the cholera patients may be divided into two large classes : those who are going to live, and those who are going to die. And only towards the last is it at all possible to decide in which class to include the patient. The same curious characteristic which distinguishes the epidemic itself, is also discernible in the patient's case. We are at a loss to understand why one patient dies after a few hours, another after a day or two, whilst the third recovers, notwithstanding the fact that the disease has developed itself with precisely the same symptoms, and, as far as one is able to judge, with precisely the same virulence in all three cases ; why one patient, who seems to have been but slightly attacked, should suddenly fall into the agonies of death, whilst another, who lies in the last phase of cholera, and

whom the doctor has already made over
to the priest, should unexpectedly recover.
We stand here on unknown, untrodden
ground ; the usual indices, the patient's
power of resistance, age, etc., all are at
fault in this case.

And whatever may have been said concerning cholera and other contagious diseases, that the virus loses its intensity with
the actual decrease of the epidemic itself,
that the cases towards the end are of a
milder character—I cannot see that the
argument holds good here. The cholera
at the present moment is decidedly on the
wane, in spite of which there are a number
of these *foudroyant* cases every day.
For instance, yesterday, during the morning
inspection (at eight o'clock), seven cholera
patients were received at the Santa Maddalena Hospital, all seven had been perfectly well the previous night, and by ten
P.M. six of them were already dead. People
are now being struck down in the streets,
just as they were during the worst days of

the epidemic, and the man who drove
me out to Granatello day before yesterday, fell off the box whilst waiting
for me, dying four hours later — the
poor fellow never got his fare after
all.

And it was just the same last year in
Egypt, when the cholera was supposed to
be extinct in Alexandria ; after twelve
days, during which there had not been a
single case at the cholera hospital, the
disease returned with the same virulence
in the case of one of the French doctors,
poor Thuillier, who was roused at three
o'clock one morning by the first symptoms of cholera, and about whom at
eight o'clock the news had already been
telegraphed to Paris that he was at
the point of death ! True, that as far
as he was concerned, a sort of artificial life had been kept up for about
twelve hours, but it was absolutely useless,
and almost cruel under these circumstances, where the extinction of life is not

synonymous with ceasing to *live*, but with ceasing to *die*.

As I write Thuillier's name I am reminded of a graceful act of Dr. Koch's, the celebrated German savant. Koch happened to be in Egypt at the same time as the French doctors, pupils of Pasteur, who had been sent out by their Government to study the cholera question. As is well known, Koch and Pasteur have come to close quarters on many a scientific battlefield, and the discussion has been carried on with a vehemence of which the origin, alas, can be traced to political animosity; for Koch, no matter how great a man, is nevertheless *le Prussien* in the sensitive Frenchman's eyes. Even in Alexandria some latent enmity existed between the French and German emissaries. The great German experimentalist had a fine opportunity of proving that the echo of these slight differences dies away when face to face with death, and that the grave is the neutral ground on which all men meet. Dr. Koch was present when the French physicians laid their colleague in the grave, and in his own name and that of the other German doctors, he laid two laurel wreaths upon the coffin—"they are simple," said he, "but still they are made of laurel—they are those we offer heroes!"

I wander from my subject, but Koch's name is so intimately connected with everything concerning cholera, that I may almost be allowed to do so.

E

V

PROPOS of doctors, as I said before, many of the Neapolitan physicians had remained at their post from a sense of duty, whilst others had thrown themselves into the fray stimulated by a certain amount of scientific interest. But there is a third sort of physician out here, and it is impossible to include him in either the former or the latter series, *i.e.* the runaway. And he deserves a special mention, but I will spare him here. That society will bear him in mind for some time to come, I think I may safely venture to affirm, after what has just happened in the case of a Neapolitan gentleman of some standing

in the town.   Whilst all his colleagues
had looked upon it as their duty to remain
on the spot, and lend every possible assistance in their power, he had kept away,
excusing himself in a public letter [1] from
returning to the town, on the plea of family
matters!   He took this opportunity of
mentioning that he was an excessively
courageous fellow, and as a proof thereof,
he modestly reminded those of his oblivious
countrymen who dared to question his
heroic attributes, that "alone with six
bersaglieri he had taken a cannon from the
Austrians at Villafranca."   But this was
not of much avail—time seems to have
somewhat rusted the cannon—and the tide
of popular feeling rose so high, that he
was requested to resign his appointment
without further delay.   The matter grew
so serious that at last he was compelled
to put an end to his *villegiatura*.   He
came back on Thursday and found that it
would be impossible to regain the people's

[1] Printed in the *Piccolo* newspaper.

confidence, unless he reported himself that very day as volunteer "*infirmier*" at the cholera hospital.   As was to be expected, this new act of heroism was immediately advertised ; the "Villafranca cannon" was again lugged out of its arsenal of oblivion, and dragged with rattling phrases across the columns of every newspaper in the town, pouring great broadsides into all those who dared to entertain a single doubt as to the worthy gentleman's courage,—and public opinion was again satisfied.   Such are the *galantuomini*, the so-called better classes out here, ostentatious and ridiculous.   I hold more and more to my poor lazzaroni, who are far more interesting as a study, and infinitely more sympathetic in themselves.

It irritates me to think that they actually complied with his request to be allowed to play the *rôle* of infirmier at the cholera hospital.   No doubt it was a convenient platform on which to enact a reconciliation scene with his discontented

fellow townsmen, but in my opinion far
too solemn a place to desecrate by such a
farce. (The director of the hospital is
nevertheless a very able man, and a member of Parliament into the bargain ; here,
as in France, the medical faculty furnishes a
number of representatives to the Chamber.)

The Villafranca hero (he is also a
colonel of the Reserve Force) is now and
again to be seen up at the hospital. He
absolutely reeks of camphor, which is, I
suppose, his ideal disinfectant. He often
slips out into the corridor or into the
garden, where fearless friends or newspaper reporters are to be found paying
their tribute of admiration to his infirmier's costume. I wonder if it ever strikes
him that he ought to be proud of being
allowed to wear the simple gray blouse,
which is perhaps more deserving of
medals than the gold-laced coat of his
colonel's uniform ! I know some one who
saw him the other day helping to put one
of the cholera patients into a bath, and it

seems that, according to all appearances, the gloved infirmier might have been handling nothing short of a fiery shell itself. . . .

If he would like to know how heroes conduct themselves in battles such as these, let him go into the next room where lies Sœur Philomène, the brave sister of charity, who, without flinching, has nursed the cholera patients day and night ; she has fallen at her post, and now lies calmly waiting there for death.

It is a different sort of courage to that with which cannons are taken that is required here——the silent, unsung courage which Napoleon, the great taker of cannons, valued at so high a rate, the courage which he called, "*le courage de la nuit.*"

As far as the municipal authorities are concerned they have certainly done their duty during these hard times, if not at the beginning, at any rate during the last period of the epidemic. And the work that had to be got through was gigantic, it was a case of beginning from the beginning, for Naples is absolutely innocent of anything like sanitary arrangements ; I shall take some other opportunity of returning to the question of the sanitary conditions of Naples——it is interesting enough. There is no doubt that the king's visit during the worst days of the epidemic had a most stimulating effect upon the official authorities. But I am bound to admit that during these last times they have somewhat relaxed in their efforts, and I reckon this factor to be one of considerable importance in the discussions that are still going on as to the reason of the recrudescence of the epidemic last week. Fortunately the cholera did not wait for the doctors to finish their discussions, it took the matter into its own hands, and diminished rapidly. To-day the *tramontana*[1] is blowing, sweeping away a large quantity of cholera virus from amongst us, and in about a week it is my belief that the

[1] North wind.

cholera returns will be no more numerous
than they were a fortnight ago.   And it
is high time, for Naples is as near her
complete ruin as possible.

I know for a fact that a petition has been
sent up to the Home Office in Rome, for
permission to discontinue the publication
of the cholera cases, for it is a question of
life and death to Naples that the epidemic
should come to an end—officially at all
events.   A continued publication of these
cholera cases will be enough to scare
away all foreigners for the whole winter ;
and as foreigners are the only real source
of income to Naples, it is an absolute
necessity that silence should be kept on
the subject of the epidemic, and that
every endeavour should be made to forget
all about it as quickly as possible.

But in such hotbeds of infection as the
fondaci of the Mercato and Porto quarters
—dark damp holes into which neither air
nor light ever penetrates, and where so
many people, reduced to the most frightful

misery, are so closely packed together—
the cholera may easily retain its vitality
for many a day to come.

And it isn't much better in the suburbs
of Naples than in the surrounding villages.
I went again to-day to the *Bagno di Granatello*, the convict prison, situated between
Naples and Portici, where the infirm
convicts and those who are chronic in-
valids are kept. There had been several
cases of cholera during the past week,
but they had been hushed up, and nothing
had been done for the poor prisoners, of
whom the greater part are old and
crippled. The cholera patients have not
been isolated, but are obliged to lie with
the rest in the terribly small room where
260 unfortunate wretches are huddled
together. The cholera has cleared a
space for them now, for many of their
companions have died, and many will
be dead ere long. These prisoners are
human beings like ourselves, and are not
ruffians at all, their crimes for the most

part consist of smuggling, of having repeatedly deserted the coral fishing-boats,
etc.——perhaps at one time when the blood
was young and the quarrel violent, a knife
may have glistened in one of the hands
so withered now.   One can imagine the
despair of these chained witnesses of the
cholera's invasion, as one after the other
succumbs to the disease.

I went there to-day for no other reason
than that of being present during the advertised inspection of the prison.   I am still
indignant at the remembrance of all I saw
as I write these lines.   Since yesterday
there have been seven fresh cases, and
four people died whilst I was there to-day.
It would have moved a stone to have
seen the despair of the poor captives as
they kissed the clothes of the fine gentlemen around, and to have heard their
agonised entreaties for succour and relief
——it was well that I was no inspector
of prisons, for I would have thrown the
doors open to every one of them !

But the inspectors, more accustomed to the dark episodes of prison-life, were of a different opinion, and they were pleased to attest "that the sad condition of the locality itself and its overpopulation, had made isolation and disinfection impossible, rendering every other hygienic amelioration equally so."

And the long-looked for and anxiously-awaited deliverance was reduced to this, that one of the members of the committee very carefully and very solemnly filled a little flask with drinking water, drawn from the prisoners' well, to be taken up to Naples for analysis—and then they took themselves off!

But this, however, was no question of finding, or not finding microbes in the water next morning; the sick ought to have been removed that very day to the cholera hospital, and—as it was impossible to disinfect the miserable hole—all the rest ought at once to have been put under inspection in some other isolated place.

I am out of all patience with the heroes
of the day, the wretched microbes, *for
human beings are being forgotten for
microbes*.   As the actual returns were
too inconveniently high to suit the
inspectors and sanitary commissioners,
it was thought desirable to take a middle
course, and to advise the public of forty-
two cases and thirty deaths—and these
were the figures with which the morning
papers reported the inspection of il Bagno
di Granatello.

I heard in the meantime that the
member for Portici had telegraphed to
the Home Office for immediate assistance,
and I only hope, for the poor prisoners'
sakes, that the help will come soon, and
will take a more energetic form than that
of lax inspectors and microbe hunting
chemists.

A good deal has come under my notice
during these last times, but my experience
of the Granatello prison was certainly
dreadful.   The most appalling stench all

over, dark cellars, with damp, moss-
covered walls — this last is not to be
wondered at, considering that the prison
is situated at the water's edge. There
are not many people who have seen the
Bagno di Granatello, for the old building
cannot be distinguished from either Portici
or Resina. When the sea is rough, as it
was day before yesterday, when I was out
there, the water runs down the walls, and
an icy draught blows through the so-
called gloomy halls, inside which several
hundred of these unfortunate prisoners
dwell. Even one of the Neapolitan newspapers admitted that the place was one
which might be turned to account as a
Scuola di piscicoltura,[1] but was altogether
unfit to harbour human beings !

If you think that my description of an
Italian prison is altogether too gloomy,
just read one of the recently-published
official reports concerning the penal estab-
lishments of Italy, by "Commendatore"

---

[1] Piscicultural establishment.

Beltrani Scalia, a book which the newspapers speak of as "*interessantissima*," but
which, in my opinion, is ghastly.

The book fell accidentally into my
hands yesterday. I looked in vain for
anything worthy of remark concerning the
Bagno di Granatello, but on another page
the following paragraph caught my eye :
"The medical duties of the . . . prison
are confided to a barber, who is a
"bleeder" into the bargain."—Well, that
is enough, is it not ?

＊   ＊

＊

I felt I must have a breath of fresh air
after all this—I had become so embittered
inside that wretched prison, and so depressed at the idea of all the misery one
is obliged to witness in this weary world,
and which one can do nothing to relieve.
I went out to Resina, and came home on
foot.   And as I tramped along, I began
to wonder whether, after all, there might

not be something in the old legend that
maintains that we shall all meet again in
another planet, where a sort of mutual
transmigration of souls is to take place,
where all the *rôles* are to be reversed ;
where all those who have been unhappy
here below are to be happy, where the
poor are to feast whilst the rich stand
looking on, where those who have had the
lash down here are to hold the handle of
the whip in their own hands, where the
hard-hearted jailors of this world are to
sit in the cells, whilst their former prisoners
go round inspecting them ! And in that
promised land animals should be allowed
to go about illtreating human beings, all
the little birds and butterflies should fly
about on free wings, and in their turn see
the sportsmen sitting stuffed and shut up
in enormous glass cases, and all the butter-
fly catchers in long rows dangling their
legs, with long pins stuck through their
bodies—but would they be half so good
to look at as their former victims, the

butterflies? And this planet's steep hills should swarm with all the broken-winded old cab-horses, who should also, in their turn, sit on the coach-box, returning every bloody stroke of the whip dealt out to them by their former tyrants, the cabmen of this world. . . . Except that animals are much kinder-hearted than human beings, and would not care to torture the "lords of creation" for very long.

But I myself, what would become of me up in this remarkable planet?

If, at this very moment, I were to find myself translated from this vale of tears and transported thither, and my future destiny were to depend upon what I had been doing during this last period of my earthly existence, I really don't know what I ought to expect! I don't think I have had much occasion to quarrel with my fellow-creatures just lately, but I am very much afraid I might be accused of cruelty to animals. For I do nothing but torture animals all day long. Either I " catch them alive," or I bring them up with every cunning precaution by means of cultivation-tubes, feed their little ones, in just the right degree of warmth, on what they most prefer, such as Pasteur's bouillon, gelatin, etc., and all that for the sake of illtreating them as much as possible later on, for the sake of fumigating, cooking, drying, poisoning them, and afterwards peering at them through the microscope, to make sure that I have really succeeded in torturing them to death, the poor unconcious (I had almost written *innocent*, but I dare not on account of Dr. Koch) microbes, who have no idea of my evil intentions towards them! Shall I, all things taken into consideration, be turned into a cholera microbe myself, to be tortured after the same fashion by one of that planet's physicians, who shall peer at me through his gray spectacles with the same sinister intentions?

A propos of doctors, I wonder what will become of them up there? Will they by

F

any chance be made to exchange places with their former patients? That were a hard punishment!

But supposing I am not turned into a cholera microbe, what then? Perhaps I shall be condemned to sit and read in print, all the rubbish that has flitted across this poor, restless brain of mine—that would be rather too much of a good thing, I think I would vote for the microbe.

VI

ERHAPS it was stupid of me to make fun of the cholera microbes in my last letter : I really begin to think that I am wrong and Dr. Koch is right, as far as their being dangerous is concerned—at any rate the cholera microbe must be a vindictive little beast. Since last I wrote, two weeks ago, I have had plenty of time for reflection—it is astonishing what serious thoughts come into one's head now and again.[1]

It were interesting enough to write an account of the cholera in its march across the world, but I don't happen to know it by heart, have no source of information

[1] Between this letter and the last one, the author had been ill.—M. V. W.

to draw from here, where I am now laid up, and the consequence is I really have nothing to write about. Here is what I remember, and for the matter of that, it is all that concerns us for the present, as I mean to limit myself to the Neapolitan cholera—about which I do know something.

We are aware that cholera is an Indian disease, that it is at home on the delta-land of the Brahmaputra and Ganges, where it reigns as an endemic. It began to travel round the world in 1817, appeared the following year in British India, Siam, Tonquin, China, Persia, the Mediterranean coast of Syria, etc., but left off between 1823 and 1824 without having spread to Europe. In 1827 it again recommenced its march across India. . . . nay, I think we'll go no further, I have been ill, am still weak in the legs, and quite incapable of " marching" along with the cholera any longer. To cut the matter short, Naples was visited by this epidemic for the first time during

the autumn of 1836; it broke out in one
of the quarters that has been most severely
tried this time, *i.e.* Porto, spread rapidly
over the whole of Naples, and came to an
end in February 1837.

As regards the epidemic of 1884 (the
seventh since then), it is as yet too early
in the day to cast up the accounts; the
cholera is still in existence, though there
are but few cases, and it is likely to hang
about for some time to come. I do not
inclose the bulletins — they are already
well known. One need not be specially
quick-witted to arrive at the conclusion
that these figures are inadequate to gauge
the actual extent of the damage done by
the disease. There are manifold reasons
for keeping these official bulletins so low.
First and foremost, attention must be
drawn to the fact that, as long as it is
possible, the people refuse point-blank to
have anything to do with the municipal
authorities; and no one who has set foot
in the poor quarters during the days of

the epidemic will attempt to deny that many of the sick and dead of Mercato, Porto, Pendino, and Vicaria were never reported to the municipality at all. And of course this was more than ever the case whilst the epidemic was at its height, when there were neither cabs nor stretchers in sufficient numbers to transport the sick, and when the town authorities were compelled to hire the Portici omnibuses to convey the dead up to the churchyard.

Another explanation of these low figures : the municipal authorities dared not publish the real amount of reported cases, they even diminished them considerably in order to avoid a panic. The highest official entries of the sick and dead are respectively 966 sick, and 474 dead (in twenty-four hours) ; but there are others besides myself who share the belief that during not *one*, but *four or five days*, there were *about 1000 cases per diem.*

One proof of the absolute insufficiency of these bulletins can be obtained by the perusal of the reports issued recently by the "White Cross." During the twenty days' existence of this voluntary ambulance, there had not been, according to the official statistics, more than 9689 cases, and 5356 deaths—well and good, during these self-same days, *this association alone* provided medical assistance for 7015 cholera patients. If it be taken into consideration that at the same time the "Red Cross" and "Green Cross" (the other two ambulances of importance) had as many sick on their hands as they were able to attend to, added to which the medical staff of the municipality, although it had been doubled, was quite insufficient to attend to all the town cases brought before the authorities, and if the above-mentioned fact be remembered, that for a great, and very great quantity of the sick in the poor quarters *no medical assistance of any kind had been sought*—then it will easily be understood, by virtue of these proofs alone, that the official numbers were invariably below the mark, did not perhaps correspond to half the actual cases.

The people's inveterate dislike to everything concerning the municipality—which strikes us as so strange—is a fact that I shall try and explain to you another time ; I think I understand it somewhat.

If you wish to know which parts of the town have been most severely tried by the cholera, you will find that, during this epidemic as during the previous ones, the four poor quarters are precisely those in which most cases have occurred.

The expression used by the Prime Minister Depretis, *Bisogna sventrare Napoli !*[1] has become the watchword of the day ; these miserable poor quarters must be done away with, for they are a standing danger, not only to the rest of Naples, but to the whole of Italy and

---

[1] Naples must be disembowelled !

Europe into the bargain. Hotbeds more favourable to infection are not to be found in any other European city, and here the epidemic, which otherwise might possibly have decreased, takes a new lease of life with which to continue its journey. And this does not apply to cholera alone.

Strangers are always afraid of the Roman malaria, but one never hears a word about the *Neapolitan typhoid fever*—by far the most dangerous in my opinion. Typhoid fever is *endemic* out here; it is a permanent disease, which, with its large death-percentage, craves an annual number of victims, more especially amongst the new arrivals, whose power of endurance is less. And it is from these self-same quarters that this atmosphere of contagion spreads out over Naples. This is not the only malady which flourishes here; there dwells another creeping disease in these regions which is not sufficiently well known, which may be compared to the Roman malaria, and which goes by the

name of *febbre napoletana.*[1] And do you
wish to know what that is like, you need
only take a turn in the alleys and "fondaci"
of the poor quarters, and you will be brought
into contact with more specimens of this
disease than you care to see. Here never
shines the sun, but should you come upon
some corner into which a stronger light
than usual has found its way, then look
into it closely—it is there that you will
most surely discover your new patients,
for they think that is the sun, and they
are shivering with cold ! Look at the
attenuated little children as they stretch
out one hand, dry as a skeleton's, to
beg a soldo ; the little one puts the
other in his mouth for you to understand how hungry he is—if he speaks at
all it is to say "*muojo di fame*"![2] Look at
the jaundiced, faded little face in which two
large eyes are glowing with fever—and you
have a picture of *febbre napoletana* before
you. Look at it closely—but give him a

---

[1] Neapolitan fever.　　　[2] I am dying of hunger !

soldo, he needs it so sorely, he is, alas! so
often right when he tells you how hungry
he is—poverty and fever go hand in hand,
and I hardly know whether I wish *la febbre*
did not exist, it is perhaps more merci-
ful than we, for it so often bears the poor
little one far from hunger and distress up
to the pauper's burial-ground.

*　　*

*

The laws of hygiene teach us how close
a connection exists between the sanitary
conditions of a locality and the density of
its population. The history of the Neapolitan epidemic furnishes us with an
example of this law concerning density
of population. Upon a surface of eight
square kilometres (amount of surface that
has been built over), there dwell no less
than 461,962 human beings. *And according to the official statistics no less than
128,804 of these people inhabit underground dwellings and cellars.* But there

is something worse than these " *bassi* " and
" *sottoterrani* " ; another step down the
shelving ladder of society and we come
to a still more wretched form of habitation
—to the "fondaci." You have often heard
me speak of these places as the scenes of
the most appalling misery out here—I
mean to tell you what a fondaco is
when we have come to the end of our
medical inspection. There are eighty-six
fondaci in Naples at the present moment ;
formerly they were still more numerous,
but more modern constructions have done
away with a good many of them. Three
of these fondaci (in the Chiaia, S. Ferdi-
nando, and S. Guiseppe quarters) are
pretty clean, that is to say in comparison
with the others ; and as this is only a
question of *the most ghastly human habi-
tations on the face of the earth*, I do not
include these three. Of the eighty-three
remaining fondacos, the Mercato quarter
contains 13, Porto 19, Pendino 12,
Vicaria 17, and all the other quarters

put together 22. *As many as 9846 in-dividuals dwell in these fondacos*, all of whom are included in the enumerated population (a distinction which has not been conferred upon a good many of the other poor creatures—in consequence of which the figures run low).

A third sort of dwelling-place consists of the so-called *locande* where lodgers are received for the night at two and three soldi a head. (I have even seen locande where they are received for one soldo a-head, but there the people sit and lean their arms and heads *against a rope* that is stretched across the room from one wall to another, not a bad idea for accommo-dating a crowd). It is quite impossible to say how many of these locande are to be found out here ; the only statistics on the subject are of ancient date, and they report 105 locande in Porto, with space for 2793 beds ; 81 in Mercato, con-taining 276 rooms, and space for 1319 beds, etc. etc.

Fondaci and bassi I know well enough, but my acquaintance with locande is somewhat limited, although once, with a Camorrist for guide, I went over every locanda in the Mercato quarter, in order to look up an old guitar-player, a former friend of mine—I mean to tell you that story some day.

There is a fourth class of human beings here in Naples who live neither in houses, in bassi, in fondaci, or in locande—a very numerous class indeed, but they do not come into the reckoning, as we on our solemn sanitary inspection go the round of the houses, in order to calculate afterwards the extent of space occupied by each inhabitant, and the cubic metres of air exhausted by each of them per diem. No, they do not come into the reckoning, these representatives of the fourth class, but they are old favourites of mine, and they are, if not from a hygienic point of view, at all events from an artistic point of view, the most interesting of the whole lot, and that

is why they are included in my classifica-
tion of the Neapolitan poor. This fourth
class of human beings—well yes, goodness only knows they have space enough
to dwell upon, and how many cubic metres
of air they exhaust is more than I can
say, for they have the starry heavens
above them and—the sewers beneath
them.

This is the class of Neapolitan poor
who have no home at all.

What their numbers are, no one can
tell ; the individuals of which this class is
composed shun all statistics, stand entirely
outside the reach of the census. If you
want to inspect them, you must set about
it at night. Go out for a few hours when
the noise of the day is over, and you will
find them everywhere. Your foot stumbles
accidentally against a soft bundle, the
bundle moves away, and with a "*scusate,
Signorì*"—not with an oath as would be
the case at home—the poor wretch whom
you have awoken draws his legs beneath

him, and rolls himself up in his rags again. He begs your pardon because he has no home but the streets to sleep in! Beneath the lamp which lights up the Madonna's picture in the corner, on all the church steps, beneath the upturned boats at Mergellina, beside the newspaper kiosques, beside the *acquafrescaio's* stand, on the benches of every public place and garden—everywhere do you come across them ; mothers with their babes at their breast and a couple of little ones half-concealed beneath the ragged old shawl, cripples whom you will find on the same spot early next morning, in order to beg their way through the day, half-grown boys, some of them sitting alone rolled up like hedgehogs to keep themselves warm, others lying in a heap under one common shelter, an old cloak, a sail, one or two old sacks, and the like.

It is incredible how much can be stowed away under one of these old cloaks! I had been out to one of the Mercato fondaci the other night, and was going home towards morning, it must have been between three and four o'clock, it was still dark. Meditating profoundly, Heaven only knows on what subject, I crossed the Piazza del Carmine, when suddenly I stumbled against the old church steps. At the same time I trod upon something soft which happened to be lying on the ground —and in the twinkling of an eye, seven startled urchins sprang to their feet. I told them how sorry I was to have awoken them, and they laid themselves down again in the best of tempers, conscious that they had very unexpectedly earned enough to keep them going for the next twenty-four hours—"*morgonstund har guld i mun*"[1]—or at any rate copper! I, who lie awake so long before I can get to sleep, gazed wistfully at the fourteen legs as they kicked about for a few seconds under the ragged old cloak;

---

[1] Swedish proverb—"The morning hour has gold in its mouth."—M. V. W.

G

the next moment all was still and quiet—
the positions were familiar, and had often
been rehearsed—and the seven homeless
little lads slept on in peace, upon the
tumble-down old steps of Santa Maria
del Carmine.

VII

ASSISTANTS

LAST time I wrote I promised to tell you what a "*fondaco*" was. Well, I ought to have no difficulty in describing one of these homes of misery and distress, they are familiar enough to me. But now let me suggest a plan, which, if you have no objection, will suit us both equally well, for then I shall be spared the trouble of describing it to you, and you will be spared the trouble of listening to me——come and see one for yourself! I am going down to one of the Mercato fondaci this very evening to look after a patient——come! let us go together.

We begin by driving down to *Il La-*

vinaio ; no cabman cares to go further at this time of day, and it would be no easy matter to do so, for the streets have become so narrow that we are obliged to go the rest of the way on foot.

You are surprised to see how well I know my way about this labyrinth of lanes and alleys, but then, you see, I have been here so often ; we are now going through streets the names of which you have never even heard, and which you would certainly be unable to find on any map of Naples ; no stranger has ever set foot in them before, and very likely no Neapolitan either for the matter of that. However, it is not very long before I come to the end of my own acquaintance with them, but it is of no consequence, for over there in the corner, just where the little lamp is burning beneath the Blessed Virgin's picture, is the Vicolo Duchesca,[1]

[1] The cholera was fearful in this alley. According to one telegram, thirty cases were reported to have taken place in one hour alone.

where we shall find a cicerone to guide as further. Do you see the boy standing over there, holding a tiny little donkey by the bridle? It raises me considerably in your opinion, does it not, to hear that I am the proud possessor of both boy and donkey. They are the only survivors of a whole family who used to live in this street; the boy's father and mother and two sisters are lying at rest up in the *Campo Santo*. The father was a green-grocer (*verdummaro* as the Neapolitans say), and the little donkey used to trot round with him, bearing the travelling shop upon her back. But everything went wrong when the hard times set in, and then the cholera attacked him and he died up at the hospital; and a couple of days later, his wife and two other children sickened and died in their own home. I heard the sad—and alas, the usual— story that very same day from a woman in the neighbourhood, and being so close at hand I thought I would go round.

A miserable hole as usual; the little lad was sitting on the cold damp floor crying bitterly, and in the corner stood a wretched-looking little donkey who had not been included amongst the survivors. She had evidently been quite forgotten, and was almost dying of starvation, her last meal having consisted of a portion of the straw mattress, on which the dead woman was still lying.

The boy and donkey are now under my special protection. Peppino (the boy) lives with a woman in the neighbourhood, and the donkey has set up a separate establishment of her own, in the tumble-down old place which did duty for the family abode, and which is certainly more suitable for a stable than for a human habitation. I don't flatter myself that I have done much for them—it is so easy to play the *rôle* of patron here! The boy costs me four soldi a day, the donkey two, six soldi altogether; the cigars we have just lit cost eight soldi apiece—so you see

the sacrifice can hardly be called a great
one. Well yes, no doubt a good deal of
pleasure is to be got out of smoking, but
those six soldi procure me something
I like even better than that—look at the
boy's graceful limbs, look at his pretty
curly head, at the soft outlines of a face
almost feminine in delicacy, and at the
large melancholy eyes that look you
straight in the face down to the inmost
depths of your soul! Antinous must have
been just such a child at that age. We are
now such good friends, Peppino and I, that,
did I not think it would be a positive sin,
I would take him back to Paris with me.
And then you can't imagine the amount
of pleasure I have got out of the tiny,
thoughtful, melancholy, little donkey! I
certainly have not as yet contemplated
taking her back to Paris with me, but I
look after her in the meantime as well as
I am able. And she tries, after her own
fashion, to show me how grateful she is;
she grinds away like a saw (I suppose

you are familiar with a donkey's usual
way of expressing itself—I at any rate
know of no better comparison) every time
I go in to have a look at her; since I
have been ill she has found a more practical way of proving her gratitude, for it
is she who carries me about on all these
nocturnal expeditions, whilst I am still so
weak in the legs. The boy follows in
the wake, he knows the Mercato quarter
by heart, and has procured me many a
patient. You won't be able to understand a word he says, and I doubt
whether he will be able to make out your
refined Italian either; "*Iamo ncopp al
maruzzaro ?*"[1] asks Peppino. Yes, amico
mio, we are on our way to the poor
fellow's bedside—we were up there yesterday and he was bad enough then, but I
have not had a moment to give him till to-
day. Well! I mount my charger, Peppino
gives the word of command, "iaaah, iaaah !"
the donkey does a little grinding, and off

[1] "Are we going up to the maruzzaro?"

we go. I have no donkey to offer you, but your legs are strong enough, and you will not find it difficult to keep up with us; besides which, we are not going quickly, the donkey is in the sere and yellow leaf ("*è antica,*" says Peppino), and a bit of a philosopher into the bargain. Every now and again she comes to a sudden standstill, to meditate upon the "missing link"—which she will certainly never be able to account for. That there is something very unintelligible in the system of things in general, and something utterly unfathomable in life's dark riddle, is all she has made out as yet—I have got no further than that myself, and it isn't likely that either of us ever will. However, I uphold liberty of thought on every subject—besides which, she isn't the first donkey that has plunged into philosophy, and I daresay she is quite as likely to find the philosopher's stone as any one else; therefore I allow her to follow the bent of her own inspirations,

and make no objection to her standing
stock still when overwhelmed by reflections
on the subject of the missing link ; on
the contrary, I sit calmly on her back,
meditating on the prospects of my own
life, which are about as gloomy as the
donkey's. I tell you all this so that you
may not be afraid of being left behind.
As I ride along my thoughts turn involuntarily to Don Quixote—there must be
some point of resemblance, I imagine, as I
sit there, mounted on the scraggy little
animal, dragging both legs along the
ground, thin and wretched-looking myself,
as I am told on all sides. But if I am
the knight-errant, then it is certainly the
faithful Sancho who is following close
at our heels. He is by far the most
respectable member of the company, and
must come in for his share of attention,
since it is he who chronicles the day's
adventures, and signs his name to these
letters.[1]   And if you think that he

[1] When these letters were first published, I made an

has no special vocation of his own, just
glance at the basket round his neck,
we shall be obliged to have recourse to
it by and by ; do you know what it contains ? Well, you will find both wine and
brandy inside it, and if that is not sufficient to entitle him to a full description
on his own account, let me tell you that
there are plenty of other things besides—
ether, morphine, a Pravaz syringe, a Dieula-
foy's ditto, etc. etc.

The relations between him and my
gallant steed are, as yet, dashed with a
certain amount of mystification on either
side ; he is an extremely well-bred individual, who never fails to salute the
donkey in the same way his Creator
taught him to salute his own species,—a
fact which always bewilders the donkey in
the highest degree, as she evidently doesn't
know what to make of it all. They are

unsuccessful attempt to shift the responsibility of author-
ship on to my faithful companion of the last ten years,
my trusty dog Puck. I only wish I might be allowed to
dilate upon this subject.

about the same size, and she has never seen anything the least like him before ; that he isn't a donkey is about the only thing of which she is quite sure. Her lawful owner Peppino sympathises with his *protégée* in her complete inability to classify the species of creation to which this new comrade belongs, and has finally come to the conclusion that he is a "*lupo*" [1]—an opinion, moreover, which is shared by all the surrounding neighbourhood. Somehow or other I have managed to make these poor friends of mine believe in me, they are thoroughly persuaded of my good faith, and of the fact that I mean to help them as far as it lies in my power—but that the big dog who follows me everywhere is not a wolf, of that I have been quite unable to convince them. And perhaps, all things taken into consideration, it is just as well that they should think so, for he has inspired a certain amount of wholesome

[1] Wolf.

fear which has been far from useless,—
unfortunately it is only too true that
these regions are not particularly safe
after dark. But we know each other
so well now, I don't think there is any
fear of danger—besides, we hardly look
as if there was anything about us likely
to tempt the poor hungry eyes. An
empty stomach, some one lying ill at
home, for whom the doctor has ordered
good strong soup, not a farthing wherewith to procure it,—all these things are
hardly conducive to the honesty that
seems so natural to us. And that watch
and chain of yours glittering in the dark—
well, perhaps you, being a stranger, would
have done as well to have left them at
home in their case, if for no other reason
than that of exposing one of these poor
souls to one temptation less. However,
Peppino, the donkey, and "il lupo" are
watching over us; here and there the
dusky alley is illuminated by the tiny
lamp that hangs beneath the Blessed

Virgin's picture—besides, our errand is
a good one, there is no danger, believe
me, so "*avvanti!*" And if you do not
happen to be a Catholic—or a fatalist, like
myself,—above all, if your mind has been
unsettled by the daily accounts in the
newspapers relating to the insecurity and
danger of the poor people's quarter, and
the constant accidents and attacks to
which a stranger is likely to be subjected,
—then come a little closer and I will
whisper something in your ear :

"Don Salvadore Trapanese is watching
over us!" You have no idea to what I
am alluding? Well, just keep your eyes
open and look about you as well as the
darkness will permit, and you will soon
see what a powerful ally we have on our
side. The old woman sitting there in
the corner—no, it is not she who shall
solve the riddle for you, though she is
well able to do so ; see how she nods
to us ; she is one of my firm friends,
although I never could make up my

mind to become one of her customers ;
she is a vendor of chestnuts and "*chioc-
cioli*," [1] and her goods are, alas, far from
appetising——I used to give her a soldo
now and again when business was bad
(I have had some experience on that
score myself), and the cholera had just
robbed her of her daughter. Just glance
for a moment into yonder corner——the
light cast by the old woman's lantern
will help you to penetrate the darkness
——do you see that figure over there, half-
concealed by one of those projecting
doorways ? He looks uncanny enough,
does he not, lying there in wait for us,
as it were ? But you have nothing to
fear from him ; on the contrary, it is
he who will prove our safeguard. Do
you hear how he greets us——"*Buona notte,
Eccellenza !*" ? The reporter, running behind us, is the only one who refuses to
acknowledge his greeting——he growls, and
an expression the reverse of amiable comes

[1] Snails.

across his face—but that is often the way
with newspaper correspondents; besides,
there is a certain amount of reason in his
mistrust, for the fellow really has a suspicious look about him.   As you see, he is
wholly unlike the type that is usually to
be met with in the poor quarter; a long
cloak is thrown over his shoulders, he
wears his hat on one side, has a stick in
his hand, and his clothes are perfectly
good—a distinguished-looking fellow, in
fact, but a bad face for all that. Ask
Peppino—he will soon tell you who he is.
The boy looks round to make sure of not
being overheard, and then he whispers,
" *Signori, è a Camorra.*" You have read
that the Camorra is a thing of the past—
but you have been misinformed, my friend,
the Camorra is still alive ! And perhaps it
is owing to the Camorra that we also are
alive at the present moment ! The man
you saw just now occupies no high rank ;
he is not even a *masto*, he is a simple
subordinate—a *picciuotto di sgarro ;* but

he has orders to watch over us, and therefore, although we are now in the very heart of the thieves' quarter, we can go along as safely as though we were at home in our own rooms. You think that it would be as well to call for the police, but there are no policemen within a good half-hour's walk, and if you manage to come across a single official during the whole night's expedition, I will give you all my worldly goods——and the guardian-ship over Peppino and the donkey into the bargain! The only discipline in this quarter is still such as the Camorra chooses to enforce——and that is the secret that makes its existence possible. I also was under the impression that the Camorra was dead, but this year has taught me that it is still in full force, and some day I will give you a description of this wonderful institution, and provide you with an ex-ample which will show you how useful it is at times to be on good terms with the Camorra.

H

But let us get on. The darkness is falling fast around us, the streets become narrower and narrower at every step, so the donkey and I go ahead, Peppino behind (perhaps you know where an Italian donkey-driver usually holds his animal!) then you, and, last of all, "il lupo!"

The whole neighbourhood presents a deserted appearance. You ask what has become of every one. Well, you see, the cholera has been terribly busy here, and has robbed the streets through which we are now passing, of well-nigh all its inhabitants. The only living creatures about the place are a few lonely *pipistrelli*,[1] fluttering round in the thick, repulsive air, and innumerable rats, the size of half-grown cats, jumping about from one slimy puddle to the other all down the filthy street—I candidly confess I was afraid of them at first. We are now in the very centre of the poor quarter, and the dirt, which is, alas, the inseparable companion

[1] Bats.

of poverty such as this, has increased
to a degree that is almost unbearable.
You would like to turn back, would you
not? You are unable to control your
disgust at the sight of all this filth and
squalor! Well, you don't suppose that I
take much pleasure in it either, do you?
But we will push on for all that; we have
done harm enough in the world, perhaps
this is the only chance we shall ever have
of doing any good!

And then, you see, when one can get rid
of a thing so easily, the harm cannot be
great, there is not much danger in the
stains that can be washed away by soap
and water. I have dwelt long enough in
the midst of all this misery; my hands
have touched the rags of these poor
creatures over and over again—well, look
at them, are they not as clean as yours?

And when the night's hard work is over
we will do down to Mergellina, and there,
at daybreak, we will inhale the pure, fresh
air in long, deep draughts, and the blessèd

sea-breezes shall blow over our faces, cleansing and purifying our lungs, and then we will bathe in the glittering blue waters before Naples shall have awakened from her slumbers and dimmed the transparent loveliness of her crystal mirror by a single breath——and of the remembrances of last night's horrors there shall remain no single trace!

And then we shall go home and lay us down to rest, and we shall sleep like kings! And the painful memories of the night shall take the form of dreams; thou shalt dream that thou art diving deep, deep down to the lowest cave of the ocean of life, where, buried beneath the sand and slime, the shipwrecked mariners of life lie wrapped in in death's last slumber; thou shalt search with anxious eye amidst the corpses and amidst the shattered planks, to see if, perchance, one single heart be beating still; thou shalt grope about, striving to haul some of these poor drowned souls to the

light of day again——but alas, their battle
with the cruel waves is over for ever and
ever, it is out of thy power to restore
them to life again——and just as in thy
dream, it seemeth to thee that thou art
being borne to the surface, thou shalt
awaken to find the sun, the morning sun
of Italy, streaming into thy room ! Thou
shalt awaken, but thy dream shall not
have faded into nothingness, for see, thy
hands are full of shells from which the
dirt has fallen, disclosing the pearls within,
the pure pearls of the good thou hast
striven to attain, of the generous thoughts
that have passed through thy mind !
And thou shalt twine those pearls with
loving hand, into the garland of those
Italian roses of thine, whose fragrance
fills the air of a spring that never wanes ;
and of those pearls shalt thou fashion
the rosary that thou shalt clasp within thy
hand, when, like the Publican of old, thou
shalt fall upon thy knees before the God
whose wrath thou hast provoked so often !

And perhaps up in the happy fields one or two of these same pearls may find their way on to the collar that shall, some day, adorn the neck of   PUCK.

VIII

PATIENTS

WE have arrived at our destination; Peppino and the donkey come to a standstill, whilst you and I and the assistant with the basket round his neck, pass on through the arched doorway leading into the fondaco. The municipality is a good sort of institution after all, it is the municipality that pays for the fire that is burning now in the middle of the court, and lighting up the picture for your benefit—the fire is intended to purify the air, a highly necessary operation, as you will readily admit. One might fancy oneself in a cave, or, at anyrate, at the bottom of some dried-up well—this is the courtyard of the fondaco;

it is surrounded by dwelling-places, hovel upon hovel, one hole after the other, all provided with the tiny aperture that serves the purpose of both door and window. As often as not, several families live together in one of these holes, and to come across one in which less than six or eight people are gathered together, is the exception.

And what a terrific exhibition of children, eh? We have always been taught to look upon them as an expression of God Almighty's good will——if so, to what a terrible extent have not these poor starving people been blest! A child seems to creep out of every available corner, every woman has a babe at her breast, the whole court swarms with boys playing about the burning pile. A long row of children sit crouched round the fire, of which the red glow, falling across their faces, lends a sort of momentary colour to the poor little cheeks——you should see how pale they look by daylight! They do not appear to pay the least attention

to the games and frolics of the other
children, there they sit staring into the
fire like so many old people, half of them
are probably fatherless and motherless,
but all of them are down with *la febbre*.
The boy close by, who turns to greet us
with that soulless expression on his face,
and the imbecile smile which is for ever
on his lips, is suffering from spine-disease,
and has been a cripple for about two
years.   He is carried down to the fire
every evening, and told me himself that
he had never had such a good time as
since the cholera broke out.   His father is
a convict, and his mother and two sisters
died last week.   Both girls died the same
night—and well do I remember the
mother's unwitting cruelty, as she pointed to
the poor cripple—who, unable to be of the
slightest use to any one, was sitting all of
a heap on the only chair the family possessed, following us about the room with
eyes in which there was no other expression than one of complete indifference to

all that was going on around him,—well do I remember her continuous cry, "*Solo questo, il Dio non si lo piglia.*"[1] At the same time I glanced towards the cripple; the awful tragedy of the night, the sight of his sisters' fatal struggle with death, must have awakened some portion of his dormant intelligence; for, as the mother's voice fell upon his ear, the reflection of a soul flew across the faded, meaningless face, and the veiled understanding seemed to grasp the purport of her words, —he was a human being again, for sorrow had touched him, and he knew what it meant! But that did not last long, there he sits with the same soulless expression on his face as of old; and if you happen to ask him what has become of his parents, he will tell you with an imbecile laugh at every word, "*Papà è al Bagno e mamma sta al Campo Santo!*"[2] The woman standing beside

[1] "This one alone God Almighty will not take away."
[2] "Father is at the galleys, and mother is up at the churchyard."

him with the babe at her breast, has taken him into her own house since his mother died, although she herself has hardly enough to keep body and soul together.

The boy dancing round the fire over there, has lost both parents, and is now left with eight brothers and sisters; the eldest girl is sixteen years old: there she stands roasting chestnuts over the fire—the little ones are to dine off them by and by. The little fellow does not look a bit sad, he is far too young to realise what he has lost, although he is quite capable of understanding that for the first time in his life he is possessed of a decent garment, and you may be quite sure he is thoroughly enjoying the novelty of the situation. As you see, the whole costume consists of a shirt, which he drags after him, and the length of which considerably interferes with the joyous patter of his little feet; but if you look at the youngsters by whom he is surrounded, you will then understand that a shirt is an extremely distinguished garment in this part of the world, and if it happens to be a new one, such as his, it attracts considerable attention. Dozens of his small admirers are skipping about, just as God Almighty sent them into the world,—but they are quite happy for all that. The Relief Committee has provided our little friend with his new garment. A distribution of 200 shirts had taken place a few days ago, in the Piazza Mercato ; I happened to be there (not as a competitor, but simply as an eye-witness of the tragi - comic scene) — indeed there were aspirants enough and to spare, for they considerably outnumbered the shirts. The various toilettes were performed there and then, for the orders were that all the rags which presented too doubtful an appearance, were to be burnt at once. (A fire had been lit on the spot, from which the distribution was taking place, and several hundred street boys were gathered round it ; the effect of the whole scene was whimsical in the extreme.)

The same odd destiny, which at conscription time at home, presides over the distribution of uniforms intended for the new recruits, and which humorously bestows on a *small* conscript a coat just twice his size, presenting the *full-grown* warrior with another which, owing to its inadequate length and breadth, exposes the graceful outlines of the burly fellow's natural charms to full view——this same mischievous-loving destiny seemed to be presiding over the distribution of shirts in the Piazza Mercato. Great big lazzaroni, who had come up with their *omnia mea mecum porto*, and had already confidingly given over the whole of their wardrobe to the flames, stood now buried deep in thought, trying to solve the problem as to how they should stow away their great, brown bodies into the baby-shirt that had fallen to their lot ; half-grown boys tripped unceasingly over the

long baggy shirts with which the municipality had presented them, whilst tiny
babies crawled all over the ground completely hidden from view amongst the
wide folds of shirts that would have fitted
their fathers.

But let us go up to the fondaco.

There stands our patient's wife warming
a tattered old blanket over the fire—so
her husband the "maruzzaro," whom we
are about to visit, is still alive. But do
you see the way in which she answers my
silent question, she makes the sign of the
cross and points upwards—he is dead!
But why then is she heating the blanket?
"*Carmela l'ha presa stanotte,*"[1] sobs the
mother. Carmela is her daughter, she
had been so good to her father, had watched
so tenderly over him. Well, up we go!
In one corner lies the father's corpse, and
in front of it, on the floor, stand two
lighted candles, some half-withered flowers
have found their way even up here, and

---

[1] "Carmela was taken ill to-night."

lie strewn about the dead man's head.
The corpse is quite uncovered, for it was
the family's only blanket that the mother
had been warming down below for her
daughter, who must be cold, for she is
shivering so. The girl lies opposite the
wall, in such close proximity to the corpse,
that were she to stretch forth her hand,
she would be able to touch it.

Poverty, awful, incredible, unspeakable
poverty! is then the misery that follows
in thy footsteps not sufficiently heavy a
burden wherewith to have laden these
poor creatures, must they then be compelled to receive into their midst the
most ghastly of all diseases, until the very
measure of their suffering be running over!
To be reduced to taking the mattress on
which the dead father is lying, in order to
put it beneath the sick child, to be obliged
to cover, with the same filthy blanket that
has been thrown over his corpse, the
daughter who now lies struggling for life,
face to face with death in its most repulsive,

horrible aspect! No pillow to lay beneath her head, no rag wherewith to rub her, no spoon into which to pour the medicine, no sort of utensil in which to warm the wine!

And here comes the mother with the heated blanket, wrapping it round the girl with all the tenderness which a mother alone is capable of lavishing on her suffering child. She, poor mother, has watched over her husband for three nights, and this last night over her daughter, and now, exhausted with fatigue, she drops on her knees beside the bed and sobs, " *Vergine sanctissima delle grazie, salvami la figlia mia! Tu sei tanto bella Madonna mia ed ai fatto tante grazie, che queste ad una povera madre non la recuserai! La senti Madonna, come si lamenta! Dimmi che cosa vuoi da me per farla guarire? Vuoi il mio sangue, il mio cuore?* "[1]

We begin to understand something about cholera, you and I, and we shake our heads, she looks very bad, no pulse,

[1] "O Holy Virgin, full of grace, save thou my

the extremities are quite cold, and the unconscious-looking eyes are half-open.

And now to work! There is so little space in the wretched hovel that we are obliged to stand the corpse almost upright in the corner, so as not to trample it underfoot.

The only thing to be done is to restore some sort of warmth to the poor sick child ; if you can find nothing else, off with your coat, and rub the frozen limbs therewith ! And you, doctor, now is the time to make use of all you have brought with you !

And with what sympathy does not your heart go out to the poor half-dead child, how earnestly do you not watch for every favourable sign that encourages us to hope that we are on the right road, how gladly you welcome the first return of

daughter ! Thou art so lovely, Blessed Virgin mine, thou art so gracious that thou could'st not find it in thy heart to deny a poor mother's prayer ! Dost thou hear her, Holy Virgin, how she moans ? What shall I give thee to induce thee to spare her life ? Is it my blood, my life, that thou requirest ?

I

life, penetrating at last through the cold
and steel-like eyes, which tired, only half-
open, and disfigured by the deep black
rings beneath them, are slowly gazing
upon your own in the endeavour to follow
every movement! There, they grow
brighter now—it is the return of consciousness, it is the soul that has awakened! You bend over her, realising that
she has recognised you, and then you tell
her that all shall yet go well; you see
that she has understood you, and that she
wishes to speak, although she is unable to
do so. And then the lips begin to move,
and her first words are that she cannot,
will not die! You wipe the cold perspiration from off her brow, saying unto her
that she shall live! " *Si, tu guarirai, si, si.*"[1]

Then she begins to grow restless, throwing herself wildly about the wretched bed,
succumbing with the returning dawn of
consciousness to the overpowering dread of
death and pain, and crying aloud "*Salva-*

---

[1] "Yes, thou shalt live, yes, yes."

temi ! salvatemi ! ma mi salverete ! Non e vero che sarebbe un peccato se morissi ? " [1]

And then, exhausted with the heat, she cries unceasingly for something to drink. *" Ho sete ! brucio ! neve, neve ! io ardo ! "* [2]

You were prepared for all that, and have brought ice with you in the basket, and there you sit, wondering from whence the patience has come that enables you, so restless as you are, to sit there, hour after hour, dropping pieces of ice from time to time into her mouth. The large eyes meet your own so trustfully and yet so interrogatively, striving to detect in every glance, in every change of countenance, whether you are anxious, whether you still think all is going well.

And should she recover ! No one will ask to whom she owes her life. You need not expect any thanks for your tiny, tiny share of credit in the matter—and none

---

[1] "Save me ! save me ! is it not true that it would be a sin to let me die ? "

[2] "I am so thirsty ! I am burning ! ice, ice ! "

will be bestowed upon you either. The mother has her own belief that it was the Blessed Virgin, not you, who saved her child, and the more you have to do with sick people the more likely are you to come round to the mother's way of thinking. Neither are you in the humour for taking medical notes; you do not feel the least inclined to announce to the world that you have just "saved" a cholera patient, or to publish the "case" with a series of theoretical reflections setting forth the various merits of certain treatments, Cantani's, "hypodermoclys," and "enteroclys," etc. etc.—leave all that to others, or wait at least until you shall have settled down at home again, and until, in your own study, in dressing-gown and slippers, you find yourself thinking over all you have gone through.

Here you are a human being and nothing more.

Do not you disturb your peace of mind with thoughts of adorning the altar erected to the demigod of Medicine with the faded herbs of your medical experience, or of illuminating it with the tiny flame of your scientific light——there are so many crowding round it, each one trying to extinguish the other's candle, leave the care of that altar to those more worthy of adorning it than yourself! Do you go bravely up to the High Altar of Humanity, and light the little tallow candle of your slight knowledge there, and lay your simple flowers upon its lowest step; they boast no brilliant hue, no high-sounding Latin name distinguishes these flowers of yours——but at all events they have sprung from the same soil as Goethe's lines——

> "Grau, teurer Freund, ist alle Theorie,
> Und grün des Lebens goldner Baum!" [1]

---

[1] "All theories are gray, dear friend,
And green the golden tree of life."

IX

TWO PESSIMISTS

YOU recollect the little donkey I took down to the fondaco the other night, do you not? You recollect my telling you what a philosopher she was, and the way she would stand stock still every now and again, to muse upon the "missing link," whilst I turned over the problem of my own existence, not particularly easy of solution either?

Thus have we sat together for many an hour, buried deep in thought. For the last few days Rosina (for such is her name —every Italian donkey goes by the name of Rosina) has been more sociable and more communicative, the sorrowful expression

in her face has somewhat diminished, and
now and then a gentle breeze of humour
has set her melancholy ears a-flapping.
Yesterday morning we had both gone
down to Mergellina, to see the sun rise
behind Vesuvius, and whilst we sat there
waiting, I ventured—after having endeavoured to inspire her with a savoury
cauliflower — to touch upon the Past,
which I had every reason to suppose
had stamped itself indelibly upon the
little donkey's soul with many a mournful
recollection. At last I asked her to tell me
the story of her life, she should hear mine
afterwards,—she must not run away with
the idea that donkeys have a monopoly of
all the suffering in this world! Rosina
smiled bitterly, and whilst we sat there
watching the awakening bay, she let me
into the secret of her wretched life. Would
you like to know what she had to say for
herself, as she gazed over the water with
those lustrous unfathomable eyes of hers?

With gay ribbons at her bridle, her flower-decked saddle resting lightly on her shiny back, she had in bygone days borne many a smart young English miss up to Camaldoli's Convent (she was stationed on that line). And whilst the fine gentleman in attendance had tried to show off his own cleverness by insisting on the stupidity of the asinine species, she had tramped along, flapping her ears and thinking to herself, that had she chosen she could have delivered herself of quite as many platitudes as this short-eared individual, but she was too sharp for that—and the consequence was she held her tongue. And the young lady was no doubt of the same opinion, for she often patted her gently on the back with her little gloved hand, suffering her to rest awhile in order to feast upon the grass that here and there sprang up between the stones ; and from time to time she would even drop a luscious fig into her mouth.

And the donkey looked out upon the world with her pretty bright eyes, and came to the conclusion that life was very sweet, and that her older companions up in the stables were altogether mistaken in looking at things from such a gloomy point of view. " But do not let us linger over those happy days—*Nessun maggior dolore che ricordarsi del tempo felice nella miseria !*" quoth the donkey, as she described her youthful experiences—" let us get on with our story ! "

And thus a couple of years passed over her head. Conscientiously and patiently she bore her burdens up the hill, where everything looked so bright, and where she herself was often given a draught of sparkling water, and never once in coming down did she miss her footing, no matter how slippery the stones. It was hard work sometimes, " but that is part and parcel of the battle of life," thought the donkey, and forthwith plucked up fresh courage.

As time went on their care for her steadily diminished, whilst the soft down upon her back was gradually worn away by the friction of the hard saddle. One day a large wound formed upon her shoulder, but no one took the trouble to dress it, and when she tried to shake off the flies that settled upon it, they only thrashed her for her pains. But she held out bravely and did her duty patiently nevertheless, although she burned beneath the saddle. And men and women seemed to her to grow heavier and heavier, as she herself grew thinner and thinner. She, whose pride it had always been to head the cavalcade, as it wound its way up the steep hills, began to find herself in the middle, and finally towards the tail end, surrounded by those companions who held such sombre views on life in general, and dragged themselves along with heads bent low. No flowers were laid upon her saddle now, the ribbon-covered bridle was hung upon the neck of a newcomer, and after a while, a dirty, worn-out bit of leather fell to her share for ever.

Few and far between the caresses now, rarer and rarer the tit-bits on the journey, whilst heavier, ever heavier fell the whip.

"What if I returned their blows!" thought the donkey one day, as one cruel stroke after the other fell from the whip of the great lumbering fellow she bore upon her back, whilst the driver thrashed her unmercifully from behind ; but an old donkey, who was limping along beside her, tried to dissuade her—"they always manage to prove that *we* are in the wrong," said she, mournfully.

But Rosina lashed out with her hind legs for all that, endeavouring at the same time to shake off her tyrant, saddle and all. But it was of no avail, the girths were bound so fast, and during the rest of the journey they beat her more than ever. And when she got home that night, tired and hungry after the hard day's work, the manger was empty, not a drop of water was to be had, and there she was obliged to lie the whole night through, in spite of which they made her work harder than ever the following day.

That was her last attempt at kicking.

But it began to dawn upon her that the world was not the pleasant place she had imagined at the outset, neither were human beings as good as they professed to be. And thus she became bitter and hypochondriacal, inclining ever more and more unto that school in which the elder donkeys held forth their desperate and pessimistic philosophy.

One day they put no saddle on her back, but harnessed her to a great cart full of stones ; she dragged it round for a couple of years till her strength was almost exhausted, but the blows fell just as hard as ever. She wasted gradually away, lost all her interest in those things that had attracted her in bygone days, and became indifferent to the fact that no one ever decked her now—what did it matter to her that she became dirtier and more wretched-looking every day, they always beat her regardless of circumstances. Patiently and submissively she held her peace and dragged her heavy load after her, and when the whip fell heaviest she would silently raise her eyes to her tormentor's face.

And thus she fell into a complete state of decadence. One day they led her to a large square in which many of her distressed companions were gathered together; plenty of people passed by her, some of them opened the poor sore mouth, grown so sensitive from the chafing of the bridle, and examined her teeth, so worn by the dried-up straw on which she had been obliged to live—but further than that no one appeared to take the faintest interest in her. At last, towards evening, a man turned up, leading a little boy by the hand; after a few moments' conversation with her oppressor, he took her by the bridle and led her to his own home, and then she began to understand that she had been handed over to another master. She was now in the service of Peppino's father, and went round selling vegetables with him; no doubt they beat her as before, but at all events the work was nothing like as hard.

"And so on to the bitter end," finished the donkey, "till at last I thought I would really have to wind up my laborious, honourable career, by slowly dying of starvation, after having been reduced to eating up that old straw - mattress, cholera microbes and all! But then you appeared on the scene, doctor." . . . Here I interrupted the donkey with the assurance that no thanks were necessary, begging her at the same time to use no compromising titles — for were it to get abroad that a doctor was actually to be found philoso-phising for hours together with a little donkey at Mergellina, not even a veterinary surgeon would condescend to recognise him as a colleague. I thanked her, however, for her story, and felt ashamed of my own bitter thoughts,—she had a much greater right to be bitter over her destiny than I had to be over mine! And the poor little donkey had certainly every reason to meditate upon life's insoluble riddle!

And thus we got on to philosophy. She told me she began to fear she would never be able to raise the mysterious curtain which hides the future from us, and that she would die without having discovered what truth meant—"*Arcano è tutto, fuor che il nostro dolor !*" quoth she.

I had for some time suspected my little donkey of being an inveterate pessimist, and was not in the least surprised to hear her quote Leopardi, the poet of despair. I asked her if she knew anything about Schopenhauer. No, she knew nothing about him; but two donkeys of her acquaintance had mentioned him one day, after having been up to Camaldoli with two German professors on their backs— their conversation under way had turned exclusively on Schopenhauer, and the donkeys had endeavoured to follow it as closely as possible. But they had returned home more soured than usual ; they had been flogged more unmercifully than ever by their drivers, who had received no *pourboire* that day—and the consequence was, that as far as donkeys were concerned, they didn't think much of Schopenhauer. (I verily believe the sly little donkey wished to allude to the fact that Schopenhauer was as stingy as he was surly—but as I have a weakness for him myself, and did not feel the least inclined to quarrel with Rosina, I pretended not to have understood what she was driving at.)

No, according to her ideas Leopardi was much nearer the truth, the noble Italian poet whose pessimism never led him into revolting against the principle of life, but on the contrary, to resignation, to silence, to contempt; she reminded me of that saying of his: "*Nostra vita a che val? solo a spregiarla!*"

I advised her to discontinue her search after truth, assuring her, that even if she found it, she would be all the more unhappy on that account, *for truth is sad in itself!* She would do much better to cling to the illusions that adorn this life, and to make it a solemn duty to try and forget that they are nothing but *illusions*.

"But what then is the object of that process which we call Life?" cried the donkey; "if what Kant says be true, that morality is its object, why, then, it is our duty to approach this object day by day, the principle of goodness and its development ought to be seen penetrating deeper and deeper into every grade of society, and men ought to become better and better!

This, however, is not the case—all I

K

know is that the longer I live, the more mercilessly am I beaten!"

I had at first intended to take up the cudgels in Kant's defence, but face to face with this slashing argument I held my tongue, and as my eyes fell simultaneously upon her poor, lacerated back, I made up my mind to abandon the philosopher of Königsberg to his fate.

" And besides all that "——continued the donkey——" if our object in life is the continual endeavour to raise our intellectual standard, to further the development of our thinking and feeling powers, well, then we are doomed to a still greater consciousness of sorrow and sadness, for does not this very consciousness keep pace with the development of our brain, and the refinement of our nervous system ? "

" Thou'rt right enough, my poor friend," I answered, " and that is the very reason why the power of suffering diminishes the lower we descend in the scale of creation, till at last we reach the solitary calm of all sensation, where unconsciousness begins, and where life slumbers on in painless repose.

And wert thou an ordinary little donkey, Rosina, I would tell thee that thou art far less unhappy than I myself. A moment ago thou quotedst Leopardi, but dost thou remember his *Canto notturno di un pastor errante*, where a shepherd, wandering about the Himalayas, turns to the moon, condemned like himself to everlasting unrest, and takes her to witness that his flock is happier far than he himself! For animals at least ignore the extent of their unhappiness, the memory of their anguish fades speedily away, they do not know what real sorrow means!"

"The idea of asking me whether I remember those splendid lines!" answered Rosina, and forthwith the verses which I had that instant alluded to, fell upon my ears in the language of Petrarch and Dante:

"Che fai tu, luna, in ciel? dimmi, che fai
          Silenziosa luna?
     Dimmi, o luna: a che vale
     Al pastor la sua vita,
     La vostra vita a voi? dimmi: ove tende
     Questo vagar mio breve
     Il tuo corso immortale
          .   .   .   .

     O greggia mia che posi, oh te beata
     Che la miseria tua, credo, non sai!
     Non sol perchè d'affanno
          Quasi libera vai;
     Ch'ogni stento, ogni danno
     Ogni estremo timor subito scordi
     Ma più perchè giammai tedio non provi!"

"And dost thou remember La Ginestra?—

          'E tu, lenta ginestra
          Che di salve odorata . . .'"

"Thou must declaim all that another
time," interrupted I, "for see, the morn-
ing-sun is already rising over Sorrento's
hills—we must be off, my friend. We
will continue our conversation to-morrow."

"But then stones ought to be happier
than we?" hazarded the donkey, as we
prepared to be off.

"So I believe," answered I, "provided
that all life and capability of perception

be absolutely extinct,—though I have my doubts on that subject, and so had Heine, for the matter of that—and just imagine, if they be indeed capable of feeling, how much unhappier is not their lot than ours! For flowers at all events shed tears of dew, and we are able to confide our sorrows to one another, but they are condemned to silence!"

"Well, but look at idiots," ground out the donkey, "they are always happy!"

"No doubt, my little donkey, *for the power of suffering is an intellectual function*, and is directly connected with the development of our intelligence."

"Just one word more," said the donkey. "We two, who have never been particularly happy, why then, our brains must be singularly developed, and we are no doubt misunderstood geniuses, both of us!"

"No, my poor little friend," answered I, "neither of us are shining lights, perhaps we are rather smaller donkeys than some of the rest—*voilà tout!*"

X

"THE PHILOSOPHY OF THE UNCONSCIOUS"

(Something that occurred to me on returning from the poor quarter)

"WHAT was it thou wert muttering to thyself as we went home the other night?" said the donkey to me a few days ago.

"I thought I overheard the name of that well-known author who has written so extensively on the subject of poor life, who, with his harrowing description of distress, has done so much to increase the general feeling of compassion for the poor, —and the editions of his own romances."

"Ay, thou hast guessed rightly, Rosina,

but no names; we discuss everything in a general sort of way, we see things *en grand*, thou my little donkey and I.

But thou knewest well enough about whom I was thinking, about him, the celebrated writer of the new school, whose works are all 'founded on fact'; who sits there in his comfortable arm-chair at his well-appointed writing-table, running his pen swiftly over the paper. We will not disturb him, we will only watch him for a few moments—his time is very precious, his manuscript must be finished in a day or two, and it isn't so easy to limit oneself when the publisher is paying at the rate of so much a line. See, now he lays his pen aside, thoughtfully passing his hand across his forehead—the forehead wherein so many charitable thoughts abide, the hand that signs the protestation of oppressed misery against its cruel fate in so many volumes. The fixed eyes are riveted intently upon some distant object, which the busy

thoughts are in the very act of shaping—
it is to be hoped he has not caught sight
of either of us, our forlorn appearance
might easily lead him to suppose we were
beggars, and then there would be an end
to our observations,—he does not approve
of beggars. He is a theorist. Rousing
himself suddenly he begins to wander up
and down the thick-pile Persian carpet—
what can he be thinking about? Ah! I
have it! There has already been some
talk about a certain new novel that is to
see the light of day ere long—that's what
he is brooding over. The book is said to
be harrowing in the extreme, full of the
most distressing scenes gleaned from the
lives of the poor. *Le clou*, the culminating
interest of the book, is to centre in the
touching story of a mother who dies of
starvation with her babe at her breast.
It is this very chapter which he is now
revising, and which, according to all appearance, is giving him such a world of
trouble. He paces up and down the room,

his nerves strung to the utmost, talking to himself, and stopping short every now and again to dot down a few notes on the margin of his manuscript. Let us see what he has to say for himself, and take a peep over his shoulder at those memoranda of his."

"The youngster must be done away with—it is absolutely necessary,—that is what the whole plot hangs upon!

I've worked up the mother to my entire satisfaction ; that scene where the light falls upon 'the countenance that anxiety and distress have rendered unrecognisable' (*Mem. ! but on which the traces of rare beauty were still discernible*) is excellent ; but the youngster, the youngster !

She *must* be found holding a dead baby in her arms, it simply doubles the pathos of the situation, and the child must appear to be sleeping.

(*Mem. ! trade as much as possible on the mother's desperate agony, which has betrayed itself in the convulsive embrace with which* she has strained the child to her breast. *Mem. ! latter removed with considerable difficulty.*)   I have two or three different sorts of deaths at my finger-ends—we modern authors are obliged to read up everything, medicine into the bargain—but I cannot quite make up my mind whether this death from starvation, *which is what I hold to most, will allow* the brat to look as if he had merely fallen into a deep sleep !   And this new book of mine must be absolutely faultless as regards the minutest details of this description, for I let it be understood in the preface that the distressing story is not only a *true* one, but one that has come under my own immediate notice.   But how the devil is a fellow to know what a youngster looks like who has just died of starvation !"

Here the donkey grinds into my ear : " He should have come down with us to the Vicolo del Monaco this evening, and then he would have had an excellent opportunity of judging for himself."—" Be quiet, Rosina, and pay attention—this is all extremely interesting in case we should ever go in for novel-writing ourselves."

The celebrated author cuts short his peregrinations, pulls up before the great marble chimney-piece, and pokes the fire.

" Were it possible to allow of the child being *frozen to death*, it would simplify the whole thing. I know for a fact that people *do* fall asleep under such circumstances, but it is out of the question in this case, as the scene is laid in Italy, and it is summer time into the bargain, (*Mem. ! corpse surrounded by a few rose-trees in full bloom, nightingales ?—something might be made out of this !*) —though, hang it all ! I should be repeating myself, there would be a certain amount of monotony about it, seeing that no less than three children were frozen to death in my last novel.

How to despatch this wretched child into the next world is really worrying me out of my senses. The medico-legal handbook maintains that the vitality of children at the breast is something extraordinary, and that they are able to exist for several days together without food of any sort. What if I were to hurry up the mother's death by a week or so, postponing the discovery of both corpses till the child has had time to die, according to the medical authorities—ah! but then the mother would be *too far gone;* there would be no more poetry about the corpse, and I should be obliged to bar the whole of that telling scene where Rudolf, throwing himself beside her, kisses her (*Mem.! cold lips!*) No one feels inclined to kiss a corpse of several days' standing!

No, that scene must remain untouched —it is unique—there isn't a man alive who could have written anything to touch it; the whole of modern literature contains nothing to equal that passage in which Rudolf cries, '*O cruel and inexorable power that art nought but fate, blind fate; may I not ransom her dear life with mine own,*

may not her closèd eyes be once again
allowed to . . .'"

(Here the donkey took to grinding so
sardonically and noisily that it is still a
matter of astonishment to me that we
were not overheard; but when authors
are in the act of declaiming their own
works, they are capable neither of hearing
nor seeing.)

"I am delighted with the description of
the corpse, I believe it to be quite complete (eleven pages are dedicated to the
shade of the face alone). No one can
beat me at a corpse—no one!

What a pity it is I cannot make up my
mind to inspect one for myself, my intense
dislike to anything of the sort is really most
unfortunate, as corpses figure so very successfully in these sort of pictures, and are
no doubt one of my strong points. And
I don't believe that any one, as far as my
handling of the subject is concerned, will
be able to find fault with a single detail;
besides, I have again consulted my new

handbook, and am fully persuaded that no alteration is necessary."

"What sort of a handbook?" asked the donkey; I pointed silently to the book-case, whereon there lay a

" Handbook
of
Anatomy, Physiology, Pathology, and
Therapeutics for the use of Novelists and Poets,
followed by a
supplement containing in alphabetical order
a full description of all the various
deaths suited to fictitious and
dramatic purposes."

"But the youngster! the youngster! To suppress him altogether, is out of the question, the whole plot would fall to the ground, the exchange of the two infants by the bribed nurse, the mark upon the child's arm, which eventually leads to the discovery of the rightful heir."

("That is an old story," ground out the donkey, who was no doubt a novel reader herself)—

" No, the child must live, must die, and what is more, must die now, as the tragic element in the story unhesitatingly demands."

Just as our author reaches this point, he is interrupted by the entrance of a foot-man, bearing a message from the *chef*, to the effect that the soup was growing cold—the dinner-bell had already been rung twice.

Such is the force of inspiration, such are the giddy heights to which the soul of man is sometimes borne upon the wings of idealism, that he has actually been known to forget his rapidly-cooling soup! But ecstasies such as these cannot possibly last long, and the author wends his way into the dining-room, where we slip in after him. Nothing particular occurs during the meal, silently and reverentially our genius devotes himself to his dinner, a dinner upon which the starving family might easily have been kept alive for a fortnight. But the *pâté de foie gras* has hardly been served before he again begins talking to himself: "the more I think of it, the more I hold to the idea of starving them to death—it is not only original, but effective into the bargain, and there are few passages in contemporary literature that come up to that death scene of mine!"—("Are they all equally modest?" asked the donkey.—"Yes," answered I, "every one of them;") "if the thing cannot be managed any other way I must just dash off something like this at the beginning of the sentence: '*Strange to say*, the child, according to all appearances, had not survived his mother more than a few moments.'

"(*Mem.! child naturally delicate, mother utterly exhausted by previous suffering, and incapable of nursing it herself, child ill towards the last—of what?*)"

And dinner over, he goes back to his study, the busy author—towards evening he devotes himself to another work, a sea-story, in which a ship goes down with all hands, except a little cabin-boy and a Newfoundland dog. The dog howls so piteously and miserably through the night, that he is overheard by fishermen on the coast; but the sea is rough, and no one will venture to the rescue—"*what was he but a dog after all!*"

Here the author smiles complacently to himself; he sees the tears start to the eyes of every lover of dogs, as he reads the account of the poor beast's death-struggle, and the final words, "*What was he but a dog after all,*" fill him with entire satisfaction.

The surviving cabin-boy must of course be rescued, for he is the illegitimate son of a very great personage indeed, who, in order to get rid of him, has shipped him off to Australia; he is to return after a while to revenge himself, etc. etc. Of course he is driven out to sea by the wind, and is left for twelve days without a morsel of food. . . .

Here the author's pen stops short—

"let me see, twelve days without food of any sort ; is not this a trifle too long according to the handbook ? "

The cabin-boy, of course, lives upon the fare with which novelists are in the habit of supplying their shipwrecked victims, *i.e.* shoe-soles and leather straps, and, of course, the sentimental tortoise, who, out of sheer compassion, lays herself upon her back and allows herself to be caught, is likewise introduced upon the scene—but twelve days ? He cannot possibly be allowed to have any wine about him (salt water is the only thing put at his disposal), for the wreck occurred at midnight, and as the ship went to the bottom at once, there was no time to collect provisions ; but something or other he must have to fall back upon, to pull him through those twelve days !

Buried deep in thought our author lights his Havannah cigar—and whilst he puffs the thin blue smoke across his manuscript, he allows the poor little castaway to discover a packet of tobacco at the bottom of the boat.

* *

*

Oh ye authors, who in thrilling and high-flown romances portray the lives of the poor, you need not draw on your imaginations in order to describe the misery of this world, you need not strain after "effects" or search after a combination of appalling situations, you need not shed a single artificial tear over fictitious sorrows! Go back to the "old school," when pictures were not painted in the studios after hired Paris models and dressed-up lay-figures, when artists went straight to the Nature they wished to paint, and authors lived amongst the people they wished to describe!

Go out among the poor, look their misery straight in the face, and lay your hands upon their rags and tatters! And you will bear witness to the fact that

there is no romance so stirring, so thrilling
—and so heartrending as Life's great epic!
And you will blush at the remembrance
of your own heroes of romance, you
will guard against the creation of more
poor than are already to be found in this
weary world, you will not have the
courage to allow your imaginations to feed
upon new victims of starvation and poverty,
for the sake of leading them later on to
literature's market, shut up between the gilt
covers of your own volumes, to be exhibited for money like wild beasts! The
greater the smoothness, the more remarkable the finish of the literary bars behind
which the poor imprisoned victims writhe,
the higher the entrance fee across the
threshold of the title-page on which the
publisher sits, rubbing his hands. But
the victims themselves—" the wild beasts,"
whilst you are heaping up your gold,
they roar aloud for food—but what do
you care about that!

I see, that according to Rosina, I have

rather overshot the mark in my description of these illustrious authors, and that my wholesale condemnation of their cold-blooded copying system is rather too exaggerated—but I can't help that! Have ye no pity for your models, ye celebrated annalists of the lives of the poor?

I speak as I feel, and away with all metaphors!

I have no love for you, ye sentimental chroniclers of want and destitution, ye who rant about poverty and distress at two francs a line! Too well do I know these literary friends of Naples, these enthusiastic admirers of the bay's clear waters, of the people's poetry and song, ye, who write long stories, the heroes of which are chosen from out the crowd of children who swarm in Santa Lucia, ye, who feast upon your description of the handful of chestnuts which keeps the lazzarone alive, ye, who buy your silks and velvets with the rags of the half-clothed children of whom you have drawn so bright a picture!

What has become of your poetical admiration for Italy, of your oft-repeated wish, "*Vedere Napoli e poi morire;*" has she then disappeared from off the face of the earth? Have you nothing to write in behalf of sorrowing Naples, in behalf of her hunger and desolation, you who are able to write at such length about her songs and the tinkle of her guitars? Not one appeal to enlist sympathy on her behalf, not one fond word of gratitude for all you owe to Italy, not one hand stretched out towards your fellow-creatures in distress, if only to give them a scrap of bread, ye who have so often stretched out your hands to pluck her summer roses and drink the wine of her gladness!

But there is no one to understand me— and it isn't the first time that that has happened either. It is no longer the proper thing to have an ideal, and dare to acknowledge it before the world—all our ideals have vanished before the uprising sun of so-called modern culture, and people seem to have lost their faith in them, as they have lost their faith in fairy tales.

But thou, Rosina, thou wilt surely understand me! Thou art a neglected little donkey who has realised that it is not her mission to flaunt along the sunny walks of life with all the rest, and I am a poor devil who has also been rejected as unfit to figure in the great review of Life! And now we wander up and down the dingy alleys of the poor quarter —it is not worth while to show ourselves in the open streets, we are not welcome anywhere, my poor friend! Thy legs are tired, and my head is tired also, but thou trampest along as bravely as thou art able, and I strive to make the best of the little I know in the endeavour to be of some use. No one knows whence we come, no one knows whither we are bound, and no one asks us who we are, but we get along just as well for all that. But every now and again we stand

still to philosophise awhile, and it is then
we grow so bitter, old friend ; but thou
art right, 'tis best to hold one's peace !
Thou art right with thy plaintive utter-
ances which I now regret having compared
to the grinding of a saw ! Now, do I realise
how much more lies hidden beneath the
rasping sigh I misunderstood so often, and
reach thou hither that drooping melancholy ear of thine, and I will whisper
unto thee my own interpretation thereof
in human language, and in words that
apply unto thee, even as they apply unto
me,

   " *Seul le silence est grand, tout le reste
est faiblesse !* "

*   *
*

No, there is no romance so stirring, so
thrilling, and so heartrending as life's
great epic ; but its fate is the same as that
of the Bible—there are but few who care
to read it. But hast thou once looked
through a page or two thou shalt discover

how impossible it is to lay it down ; thou readest on till the book falls from thy hands, until the advent of Death, who extinguishes the lamp by which thou workest. And how empty and tiresome do not all other books appear ! How sharp hath now thine eye become to detect the strings by means of which the writers of romance succeed in dancing their miserable marionettes across the boards of that literary puppet show which, according to them, represents life !

And how severe are not thy literary criticisms now, how bare the shelves on which thy favourite books were wont to lie ! Thou flingest them away, one after the other, their contents satisfy thee no longer, their heroes are dead, of that thou art assured, for thou hast held the mirror of truth before their lips, and no breath of life has dimmed its surface ; their descriptions of Nature are like the countries that surround the Dead Sea, where no flowers scent the air, and no birds sing, their pictures are like Pompeii's faded frescoes, which dissolve when the sun of life shines down upon them!

And neither the "old school" nor the "new school" is able to satisfy thee now—thy judgment falls as heavily on the one as on the other, thou wilt have nothing to do with either idealists or realists.

And you, ye realists, reformers of the new school, you, ye heaven-scaling Titans who in your own estimation have already reached the summit of Art's temple, who strive with outstretched hands to overthrow the spire thereof, shaped by the bravest thoughts of centuries into the likeness of a cross—you fall to the ground with all the rest!

Think you, ye modern authors, who, until we have bestowed our undivided admiration upon you, are content to worship at your own shrine, think you that your celebrated "studies after Nature," your photographs, obtained by means of all the apparatus of modern realism, are truer to life than the naïve pictures of the old " idealists " ?

You talk of a return to *Nature* in literature as in art, but you entirely forget that *Nature herself is not realistic but idealistic!* Where will you find a symphony of which the romance can be compared to the murmur of the sea, where will you find a tragedy so impressive as the vast solitude of a pine forest, where will you find a poem so pure as the silent language of the violets, where will you find a sonnet so tender as the nightingale's song about Sorrento! And where will you find a greater idealist than the sun, where will you find a more incorrigible, sentimental, old enthusiast than the moon who, at this very moment, floats the glittering interpretation of her dream across the slumbering bay!

*   *

*

CONVERSATION WITH ROSINA

Donkey : " What on earth art thou driving at with those merciless criticisms of thine that refuse to approve the works of either the old school or the new ? Are we to leave off writing altogether ? "

I : " Yes, that is about it."

Donkey : " But thou thyself art always scribbling, and often have I watched thee as, seated on a stone, thou wrotest all those letters down at Mergellina ! "

I : " I should never have expected thee to classify those letters as literary works. Their utility is so evident, their purpose so *practical*, that they ought hardly to be considered from a literary point of view.

What has enabled thee to stand here philosophising with me by the hour together, what has provided thee with the clean straw on which thou liest at night, and the fresh cabbages and lettuces on which thou feedest morning and noon ? What but these very Mergellina letters to which thou wert just alluding! And Peppino, whose transformation has surely not escaped thee — of what thinkest thou does his new suit consist? Of nothing more nor less than one or two of these self-same *Dagblads* stitched together, my friend!"

The Donkey : "If that is the case, I am of course reduced to silence."

I : "And a very good thing too, 'tis always best to be silent! And silently should we pursue our way, watching the immortal thoughts that sail like clouds above our heads, and silently should we congratulate ourselves upon being allowed to follow their lofty course from here below—but we ourselves would do well to be silent always."

The Donkey : "But if every one is to leave off writing, what is to become of critics and reviewers? A good many of my colleagues have devoted themselves to criticism,—what is to become of them?

And into what channels would'st thou

turn that immense ocean of ink which threatens to flood the newly-ploughed fields of civilisation, on which an ever-increasing number of mariners venture out for the purpose of taking part in the regatta of Fame? Boats of every description are to be found cruising about this ocean, the pleasure boats of easy, graceful diction, heavy barges of solid knowledge, toiling wearily along, laden with great blocks hewn out of hidden strata, men-of-war and inoffensive merchantmen, amateur yachts and clumsy ferryboats, etc. etc."

I: "I understand thy metaphor as regards 'the ocean of ink,' and will carry it on. Well! Yonder sits the self-elected jury —having prudently determined to remain on shore — watching the race through criticism's telescope; let us only look at the brightest side, let us endeavour to forget the boats that have run aground, all those that have collided, and all those that have foundered, and let us take for granted that thou reachest the haven of Fame, and succeedest in hoisting the flag— what then? The goal appointed by the jury is not thy journey's goal—thou hast a longer journey before thee. And after thou hast journeyed for a while, the sea appeareth unto thee to become narrower and narrower, the shores appear to draw closer and closer together, and soon thou discriest land—the isle of Immortality, thinkest thou,—not so, my friend, 'tis but the other side of the river of life over which thou'rt bound to pass. Thou who hitherto hast only looked forward, thou turnest back to gaze upon the road which thou hast just traversed, and which seemed to thee so endless. How startled art thou on discovering that close behind thee there is also land, how great thy astonishment on realising that 'tis but a little river, after all, on which thou hast been struggling for so long, till at last it begins to dawn upon thee that thy first glimpse of the great ocean will be obtained

on reaching the other side. And now do
the distances appear but short to thee;
thou who hadst deemed thyself so far
ahead of thy unsuccessful, flagless rivals,
discernest now that they have caught thee
up, are close behind thee—for they, like
thee, must also cross the stream.

And then an ugly old ferryman rows
up in a rotten boat; thou askest him to
tell thee who he is, and he answers that he
is the pilot who shall conduct thee to the
other shore where the great distribution
of prizes is to take place. Thou rejoinest
that thou'rt able to steer thy boat thyself,
that hitherto thou hast not discovered the
necessity of any landmark, that thou
would'st rather sail alone, indeed, thou
would'st return if possible. Thou askest
him if he would care to see thy medals,
thou pointest to thy waving flag, and
tellest him that thou hast carried off a
prize—but this impresses him in nowise;
he hauls down thy fluttering rag, and
hoists a black flag in its stead. And

then he bids thee step into his boat, for he has orders to ferry thee over to a place where thou shalt be detained awhile in quarantine—he insists upon the fact that thy papers are not in order, and that thou comest from an infected port. Thou art afraid of being put into quarantine, thou hast been told how strong a smell of sulphur pervades those regions, and thou remindest him that a celebrated Wittenberg doctor, whose name is Luther, has decided that quarantine is out of date and quite unnecessary — but it's my belief thou'lt be detained there all the same. And then. . . ."

The Donkey: " I am obliged to interrupt thee now, no longer am I able to keep pace with thy obscure language. What is the name of this place of quarantine, what is the name of the other shore, who is the traveller, and who the ferryman ? "

I: " Dear little donkey, thou shalt have the answer to the riddle ; we have taken

M

a few liberties with mythology, and have introduced boats upon the scene, in order to enable thee, who art but an indifferent swimmer, to accompany us on our travels. There is no need for thee to meditate upon this place of quarantine, for thou shalt surely escape it, but its name is ' Il Purgatorio '; the ferryman's name is Charon. . . ."

The Donkey : "And the river, the dark river's name ? "

I : " The river's name is Styx, my friend, —the river of oblivion ! "

XI

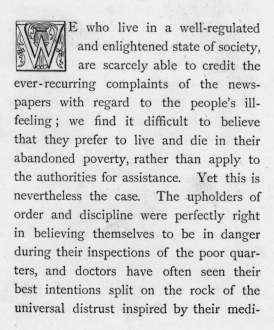

E who live in a well-regulated and enlightened state of society, are scarcely able to credit the ever-recurring complaints of the newspapers with regard to the people's ill-feeling; we find it difficult to believe that they prefer to live and die in their abandoned poverty, rather than apply to the authorities for assistance. Yet this is nevertheless the case. The upholders of order and discipline were perfectly right in believing themselves to be in danger during their inspections of the poor quarters, and doctors have often seen their best intentions split on the rock of the universal distrust inspired by their medicines and themselves. That a popular belief existed to the effect that doctors received a premium on every cholera patient they were able to report, is an indisputable fact. The idea that they were paid by the Government for the express purpose of spreading the disease, is now exploded, and I have never heard it broached save in the case of a few old men who had picked it up during the epidemic of 1836; as a rule it has been modified to the extent of believing that the town authorities, desirous of reducing the surplus population (it is in this form that the echo of the long-continued discussions on the over-population of Naples has reached the alleys of the poor quarters) had *let the cholera loose* in order to give more room! This view was universally held by the people, and was unfortunately often interpreted by acts of hostility and violence. But the very enormity of such suppositions is in my eyes sufficient to absolve the ignorant and hapless

creatures by whom they were conceived—
they are wholly irresponsible—as little to
blame for their ignorant want of confidence,
as the fever-stricken patient who tries to
turn his doctor out of doors, or the lunatic
who with delight sets fire to the hospital.

And this is why I am unable to understand how this undisguised contempt of
his medical capabilities can succeed in
wounding the professional pride of any
doctor, or how the peevish, irritable attitude of the poor people can possibly cause
any diminution of his sympathy whilst
working on their behalf. Any way it is a
good thing to be in my position and to
have nothing to be proud of—for my
sympathy has never flagged. Yet have I
never met with so little consideration as
in this part of the world, where they have
thrown my wonderful mixtures out at the
door, tried to send me after them, and
thrashed me into the bargain.

Were they to draw the line at throwing
one's medicines away, it would not be so

bad, but do you know how an old crone up at Pendino once treated me? The old lady, who belonged to the *ancien régime*, was struggling with all her might to oppose the efforts that we were making on her behalf, and was so exhausted that she was hardly able to speak; after several unsuccessful attempts, when we had finally succeeded in pouring the medicine into her mouth, she made a sign which I failed to understand, but which the *commare* at her side interpreted as a wish to speak to me. I bent over the poor old thing, who looked inoffensive enough, for the matter of that, but scarcely had I lowered my head to the level of hers—than she spat the medicine back into my face. That was her way of treating doctors, and it was certainly not worth while endeavouring to lead her benighted ideas into new grooves—so I just wiped my mouth, and we continued to be as friendly as before.

Often whilst wandering through the poor quarters, one would come across a crowd of women in front of one of these squalid little houses, some of them warming blankets and articles of clothing over a fire, whilst others knelt on the threshold in fervent prayer—a sure sign that cholera was within. To the question whether any one was ill, or whether medical assistance was required, the same churlish answer was invariably returned : " *Siete del municipio ?—qui non v'è nessun ammalato !* " [1] I soon discovered that there was nothing for it but to go in quite quietly, to look as unofficial as possible, and, above all, not to allow one's own remedies to interfere with the application of theirs. As often as not a couple of sick people were to be found within, buried, head and all, beneath everything they had been able to scrape together in the way of blankets and old clothes (the most striking characteristic of cholera, *i.e.* the rapid diminution of temperature, is

[1] " Are you sent by the municipal authorities ?—there are no sick here."

naturally what impresses the people most).
Could one help them in no other way, one
was at least able to give them a little
wine, some ice to quench their terrible
thirst, and a few soldi wherewith to pur-
chase bread for the starving family around.

And often enough as one turned to go,
the threatening, suspicious expression in
the eyes had softened, and *"Iddio vi
benedica! la Madonna vi accompagna!"*[1]
sounded kindly after one down the dingy
little street.

*   *

*

You have read in all the newspapers
full accounts of the voluntary ambulances
out here, Croce Bianca, Croce Rossa,
Croce Verde, etc. etc., you have been
informed of their extraordinary exertions,
for which indeed no praise is high enough.
It is but fair that I should mention them
in my turn.

[1] " May God bless you ! may the Blessed Virgin be with
you ! "

Yes, they have done their work splendidly, these ambulances. First and foremost stands the Croce Bianca, by virtue of its inexhaustible resources, its large stock of ready money—and its vast advertisement system. The perpetual struggle for notoriety, the continual mention in all the newspapers of its own heroic deeds, is so striking with regard to this association, that it disturbs the impression of all the great and good work it has actually accomplished. Nobody wishes to deny that the White Cross is worthy of every benediction—but after all? the whole thing is so simple it ought never to have been mentioned by any other name except its own, which is fine enough, in all conscience,—they were doing their duty, *voilà tout !*

That the work undertaken by these ambulances was no child's play, can be testified by the recent reports issued by the White Cross ; the tenth part of its members, and the seventh part of its doctors were attacked by the disease against which they were struggling. The same report contains an announcement to the effect that this ambulance has nursed 7015 cholera patients and *salvato* 3500. Happy Croce Bianca! I know doctors who have given all the help that it was in their power to bestow, and who hardly venture to assert that they have "saved" a single soul—at most murmuring to themselves at intervals "*guérir quelquefois, soulager souvent, consoler toujours.*"

The White Cross came to an end after twenty days' existence, not alone on account of the cholera's diminution, but also, to a certain degree, owing to the strained relations that had sprung up between itself and the medical staff of the town. These latter, who were doing their duty as bravely as the former, began to weary of the incessant and exclusive mention of the White Cross, and of the newspapers' continuous and undivided admiration of all its sayings and doings.

The extraordinary readiness of the press to celebrate the deeds of the White Cross is easily explained by the fact that its president happened to be one of the principal journalists in the town, the editor of the *Piccolo* (a member of parliament and well-known author, a clever fellow for the matter of that, and vastly superior to most of his vain-glorious colleagues of the White Cross).

I defy you to read a single Neapolitan newspaper written within the last few months, in which you do not come across some of these advertisements. I firmly believe that very soon there will be no inhabitant of the town who will not have seen his own name followed by a superlative of some sort, " wonderful," " superb," " heroic," etc. A chemist who, knocked up one night for a bottle of laudanum, gives it away gratis, awakes next morning to find himself famous (name, address, and everything), and the appreciative newspapers weave a

laurel wreath about his brow, quite large
enough to enable him to dispense with
the usual autumn outlay on bay-leaves for
his apothecary shop.

The wine merchant who sends a few
bottles of Marsala to the Relief Committee
is dubbed *ammirabile*, and should he refuse to take back the empty bottles will
no doubt be *ammirabilissimo*.

The lady who forwards a dozen shifts
is at once pronounced an *angelo*, and
so successfully enveloped in the flowing
drapery of these celestial beings—that it
becomes an easy matter to make over the
rest of her terrestrial wardrobe. And her
husband who despatches three pairs of old
boots—requires his own no longer, for he
is flying on newspaper wings far above
the dust of this workaday world.

One was continually told to be on the
look-out for pickpockets, but to my mind
newspaper correspondents and reporters
were far more dangerous — the greatest
amount of prudence, I may say cunning,

was necessary, unless one wished to pose alongside the apothecary's apotheosis and boot-donee's ascension into heaven. For the matter of that I was once caught myself, and it was only the merest chance that prevented me from becoming famous —a stately apparition of myself would indeed have put the finishing touch to this Pantheon of theirs.

XII

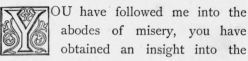

YOU have followed me into the abodes of misery, you have obtained an insight into the life of the Neapolitan poor, and have shuddered at the sight of their unequalled poverty. And you ask if it can be really true that human beings of the present day are suffered to live and die as you have seen these poor creatures live and die? You ask why they have been left so far behind the rest of Italy in its advance on civilisation and freedom?

Yes, I will tell you on whom the responsibility falls—and it falls heavily. *Nothing has ever been done for this people, nothing !*

There was a time when their degradation was convenient to the interests of the mighty, when it was considered a good stroke of policy to keep up the atmosphere of ignorance and oppression in which they breathed. That time is over, but the Italy of to-day has done no more for them than the Italy of the past, they have all lost sight of Naples in their beneficent reformation. Now every one has a stone to throw at the people's ignorance and mistrust—but they all forget that nothing has ever been done to remove this mistrust, that no hand ·has ever been held out to raise them up to better things.

Would that I were able to proclaim these words so loudly, that the sound thereof should travel up to Rome—*it is a disgrace* to Modern Italy, this complete forgetfulness of the Neapolitan people. It admits of no excuse. Every one has long been aware of the appalling misery that reigns here, and schemes for its immediate alleviation have been lying ready for many a day.

Ever since 1860 the municipality of Naples has been studying the question. Committees of thoroughly competent men have drawn up plans for the reconstruction of the poor quarters; I have seen eight of them myself.

In 1871 there was a public competition of projects for the reconstruction of old Naples, and the amelioration of its miserable sanitary condition; to my certain knowledge all the competitors were presented with medals, four of them received a reward of 6000 lire, and two others received 3000 lire. But the result? Yes, as the years succeed each other, the dust falls thicker and thicker upon the laboriously-constructed volumes that lie slumbering within the archives of the municipality, and *nothing has been done.* For want of means, think you—not so, for in the meantime the aristocratic quarter of the town has been rebuilt at enormous expense, public gardens and large squares have been laid out for the benefit of the rich. Bianchina Carraciolo, Rione Amedeo, Via del Duomo, Galleria Principe di Napoli, have all been built, and a sum of 300,000 lire is the annual subscription that has been voted towards the San Carlo theatre. The people have been kept quiet by means of the *Banco di Lotto*,[1] which is to them what the gin-houses are to our people at home. And whilst the rest of Naples rejoices in her lovely gardens and well-lit streets, the poor people's quarter has been left to its fate ; here the people live as before, and now the cholera has entered their wretched homes and done its work of destruction with appalling success. Here grow apace the seeds of virulent disease, here does fever ferment in the swampy alleys. Here do the miserable children, fearful of the light of day, grow up without care for their bodies or culture for their souls, in complete ignorance of either good or evil, here sin loses its

[1] Lottery bank.

N

guilty character, here a man hungers for
a while and then turns thief, here do the
Camorra and vice seek their recruits, and
here die these sullen and degraded beings
in the same state of mental darkness as
that in which they have lived! But here
also amidst unheard-of suffering and untold
woe, hatred of the rich is fostered, here
do the threats of the oppressed accumu-
late, here does the dagger glitter beneath
the rags!

And remember that, notwithstanding
the degradation of this people during
centuries, it has nevertheless proved itself
capable of rising up in arms when ex-
asperated by the heavy yoke of its
oppressors, remember that the poor of
Mercato and Porto have shaken the founda-
tion of a mighty throne, though stones
were their only weapons, and a simple
fisherman from Amalfi their only leader![1]

*   *

*

[1] Masaniello.

Has it ever struck you in looking at a Neapolitan woman, that however miserable her home, however ragged her personal appearance, she nearly always wears some pretty pearls or corals round her neck or in the braids of her blue-black hair? It is even so with this people of whom she is the daughter—there is something about them that defies complete degradation, that has survived centuries of misery and oppression. It is the inheritance bequeathed to them by the ideal beauty of the life of Greece and Rome.

And even now you meet, midst dirt and filth, types that bear the stamp of beauty on their brow, even now amongst the younger women, who like beasts of burden pass before you with heavy weights upon their heads, you come across living models of the ancient Caryatides, even now amongst the fishermen of Mergellina you can trace the noble head of the imperial Julian dynasty, even now amidst the children at play you discover the Grecian profile of Antinous, with the thoughtful brow and dreamy eyes beneath, even now you may see a lazzarone drape himself in his ragged cloak, even as Cæsar draped himself in his mantle, as he fell by Pompey's statue!

And in spite of all the defects that characterise this people, one is sometimes struck by a certain nobility, a certain magnanimity which reminds one involuntarily of days of bygone splendour—it is as though one stood inside the Roman Forum, where amongst the unsightly and insignificant modern houses, the eye falls upon the columns of crumbling temples and imperial arches of triumph!

Yes! it is easy enough to laugh at the people's ignorance and dark superstitions —but I have never felt inclined to make merry over it, I have witnessed too much of this silent misery, silent because it is unable to tell its woes in the language of our nineteenth century civilisation.

I always feel as if I had stepped

into another century when I am with
these people, on whom modern development appears to have had no influence for
either bad or good, where even now-a-
days the veil of mediæval mysticism
shrouds their understanding. And yet
even this mediæval darkness has its
bright side, the eternal stars pierce the
gloom of even such a night as this—
even here the little lamp beneath the
Blessed Virgin's picture shines lovingly
upon the kneeling poor, here glows even
now the beauty of the monastic life of
bygone days, in the silent charity of the
much despised monks, as they wend their
way from house to house. Call it if you
will crass superstition on their part, and
idiotic sentimentality on mine, granted
that the devotion of a handful of monks
is unable to wipe out a single item of
the long list of debts contracted by the
religious orders—I am deaf to all your
reasonable arguments, I remember nothing
but what I have so often and often seen

for myself during these last few weeks,
I remember nothing but the consolation
they bring with them, the despair for
which they have a remedy, the agony
which they are able to soothe! And
again I raise my hat to the poor old
monks—and I do so with regret, for it is
to bid them farewell. I am just about to
leave their country, their time will soon be
over, and who knows whether they will still
be here, if ever I return at some future date?

Yes, I am to start this very evening.
I am nothing but a truant schoolboy
after all, and now has Duty, the stern old
schoolmaster, come after me, birchrod in
hand, to drag me back to my everyday
work. I told him I thought it was
Sunday, I had felt so devotionally inclined the whole time, and on Sundays
no one is expected to go to school. But
I had evidently made a mistake, for he
answered that we had got no further than
the middle of the week. And then the
severe old pedagogue asked me if I had

any recollection of all he had tried to
drum into me with such infinite pains ;
and before I knew where I was, he was
examining me in geography, and asking
me if I happened to be aware that there
was such a place as Paris in the world.

And then he scowled at my slouched
hat and airy summer suit, and requested
me to be so good as to put on my frock-
coat and top-hat, and bid farewell to the
lazzaroni, farewell to the philosophical
donkey, farewell to the bay, farewell to
Vesuvius, farewell to the summer, farewell to the roses beneath my open window ! Farewell to the cholera——no, that
he did not insist upon, I was merely to
say *au revoir*, I should see it again in
a day or two.[1] Had he caught sight of
my scribblings, he would certainly have
obliged me to bid a long farewell to the
Dagblad——but he hasn't the least idea of

[1] The author was obliged to return to Paris, where he
practises, on account of the sudden outbreak of cholera
there.—M. V. W.

their existence, and you must help me to conceal them, or I shall certainly be plucked next time I go up for examination. Farewell to you in any case, my readers——we will part as we met, without exchanging visiting-cards, not so, it will not matter to you, and is more agreeable to me.

But who are the friendly authors of the many letters which I have received here? The anonymous hand that forwarded so large a cheque " to be distributed amongst my poor patients," to whom does it belong? They themselves are unable to acknowledge its receipt, for none of them know how to write ; but, believe me, you have done a good work whoever you are !

Yes, even though I be birched for having run away from school to come here, even though I receive nothing but bad marks——I shall never regret a thing I've done, no, not even the letters I have written home.

For a few of these hastily-scratched

epistles are enough to build a fishing-boat, two *Dagblads* (the *Dagblad* is a big newspaper, you know) are quite sufficient to manufacture a sail, Rosina, the donkey, if you still remember her, will live upon printer's ink to her dying day, Peppino and dozens of other hungry urchins have profited more by the *Letters from a Mourning City* than all the other subscribers of the *Dagblad* put together.

Have you any doubts now as to the "signal importance of the press for the benefit of society!"

These three Letters were written under calmer circumstances after leaving Naples.

XIII

HOW PUCK WAS LOST

" . . . the firmest friend,
The first to welcome, foremost to defend."
LORD BYRON.

IT had become quite dark inside the old church of *Santa Maria del Carmine*, here and there alone did the light of a wax-candle fall upon the kneeling poor who had just one more sorrow to confide to the Blessed Virgin, who wished to invoke her powerful assistance just once more against some trouble, to implore her, just once more, to grant some peace unto their weary souls.

Santa Maria del Carmine is the church

of the poor people, and the poor people
were well aware that now, more than ever,
did they stand in need of the Blessed
Virgin's help.   A few of them had timidly
ventured up to the wonder-working crucifix which human hands had been unable
to destroy, and which was better able to
protect them than San Gennaro himself,[1]
but most of them stood beneath a side
arch, whilst others deemed themselves
unworthy of drawing nearer than the door,
where humbly gathered together, they
kissed the threshold of the Blessed
Mother's sanctuary.

The bells rang out the Angelus, and
with a profound obeisance, one after the
other got up to go.   The doors were just
about to be closed, and I walked slowly

[1] Here is what the sacristan will tell you about this
crucifix.   During the bombardment of Naples by Alfonso
of Aragon in 1439, a bullet pierced the window above
the high altar and went whizzing through the air in the
direction of the crucifix, but the image bowed its head
and the bullet lodged in the wall.   At the same time
Alfonso's brother fell to the ground mortally wounded by
a bullet which struck him on the head.

down one of the side aisles. At that
moment a man entered the church, he
fell upon his knees, his lips moved
hastily in earnest prayer, over and over
again did he make the sign of the cross,
and repeatedly and despairingly did he
strike the ground with his forehead. As
the sacristan came up to lock the door,
he rose, threw his cloak over his shoulder,
and hurriedly left the church. Just as I
passed the spot where he had knelt my
foot stumbled against something, and I
heard a metallic sound ; I bent down and
took up a long Calabrian dagger which
lay upon the floor. We two were the
last to leave the church, and I caught
him up outside on the piazza. He
started as I handed him the knife, hastily
snatching it out of my hand. His face
was deadly pale, and there was a strange
uncanny expression in his eyes ; I was so
much struck by his appearance that I
could not resist telling him that I had
seen him in the church and that I felt

sorry for him. He looked at me grimly for a moment, and then he muttered through his clenched teeth: *"cholera in casa!"*

I told him I was a bit of a doctor and pointed to the case of instruments under my arm, offering him my services at the same time, in case he thought they might be of some use, but he shook his head and walked away.

I lingered on the piazza for a moment or two, ruminating as to what the next move should be, whether, on the whole, it were not best to go straight home to bed—I had been hard at work all day, and happening to pass the quiet old church had gone in to rest there for a while.

Just as I was about to take myself off, I saw to my astonishment that the cloaked fellow was making straight for me.

" *Siete forestiere?* "[1] said he curtly.

"Yes," I answered.

[1] " Are you a stranger?"

"*Non avete niente a fare con Il Municipio?*"[1] he went on.

"*Niente affatto*,"[2] answered I.

"*Volete venire con me?*"[3] was his next question.

I asked for nothing better.

We went down the *Via Lavinaio* and turned off into one of the narrow streets behind the little church of San Matteo; for some time I had a very fair idea where we were, but little by little I ceased to recognise the neighbourhood, and ere long was quite unable to make out in what direction we were tramping along. Once or twice I inquired after the names of the streets, but he did not answer. At last it became quite dark and I began to wonder what the time was, but none of the poor devils we came across looked as if they were likely to be possessed of watches, though I must frankly own that plenty of

---

[1] "You have nothing to do with the Municipal authorities?"
[2] "Nothing at all." [3] "Will you come with me?"

them looked as if they would have liked to have one. It is always best to leave one's watch at home on these occasions,— to wear one is not fair on those inhabitants of the poor quarters with whom one is brought in contact,—it only tends to rouse their evil instincts.

But no one even hazarded an uncivil word, once or twice it seemed to me that they actually made way for us, whilst every now and again a sort of mutual greeting was exchanged between some of them and my companion ; that is to say as far as I was able to see by the uncertain light that fell from the little lamps that hang at every street corner beneath the Madonna's picture.

We went through a vaulted passage and emerged into a little alley, so narrow that we were hardly able to walk abreast. All of a sudden the fellow asked me if I knew where we were, and I answered with perfect truth that I had not even the remotest idea what part of the town we

were in. Shortly afterwards we halted
before a wretched tumble-down house,
which, according to all appearances, was
quite deserted, although I heard him
address some one within whom I did not
catch sight of. But what amazed me
most was the fact that I could not understand a single word they said—I who had
flattered myself that my knowledge of the
Neapolitan dialect was vastly superior to
that of many a native of the place! A
man came out of the house, all three
of us went down a pitch-dark passage,
and I heard the door close with a bang
behind us. My companion took me by
the hand, which was just as well, as I was
unable to see an inch before me. We
then crossed a yard, and finally pulled up
before a miserable little hovel, from which
a faint light was glimmering through the
closed and tiny window. I could not help
thinking that the sort of adventure with
which this was likely to wind up was
only possible in Naples, or in the pages of

O

some melodramatic robber-story; and certainly the man who came forward to light us up the steps might easily have posed anywhere as a bandit's model.

More conversation ensued between him and my companion, of which, in spite of all my endeavours, I understood nothing. I just managed to distinguish the word *misericordia*, which occurred several times, from whence I concluded that he was giving an account of our meeting in the church; that *misericordia* meant *knife* in the language of the Camorra, was a piece of information I had gleaned from Peppino.

The man then raised the lantern to the level of my face, and scrutinised me closely for a minute or so, but I could not make out whether he liked the look of me or not, for he said nothing.

We were now standing in front of a half-open door, my companion made the sign of the cross, and silently we entered.

It was the usual scene. The mother lay upon the floor before an image of the

Blessed Virgin, wringing her hands in despair, and at some little distance two or three other women knelt in earnest prayer. All of a heap beside the fire, sat an old and crippled woman, muttering to herself in a weird, sing-song voice, a string of disconnected words that sounded more like incantations than prayers—I heard afterwards that she was *la nonna*, and that she was not quite in her right mind.

No one stood beside the bed ; the patient was, as usual, fighting alone with death. (The Neapolitans of the lowest class are as a rule afraid to touch a dying person unless it be absolutely unavoidable, they remain in the room but always at a certain distance from the bed.) Whilst the one man stood in the doorway, the other from *Santa Maria del Carmine* and myself went up to the bed. I took the lantern out of his hand, and as the light fell full upon the livid little face on the pillow, the stalwart fellow beside me shuddered, and then I felt that it was his own child we were gazing upon. It was already half-cold and quite unconscious. Surreptitiously, under the blanket, I administered an ether-injection, after which she rallied, as is often the case, and though the improvement of her condition was merely transitory, it nevertheless succeeded in softening the suspicious eyes around me. The little girl now opened her eyes and began to moan softly, whereupon they all gathered eagerly round the bed, alternately watching her and myself. The mother, who in her blind despair had not even noticed our arrival, rose hastily from the floor the moment she heard the child's groans, and half beside herself, began to help me to rub her with the blanket.

Just about that time I used to make a trial of intravenous injections. I had administered just such an injection that very day and happened to have my instruments with me. Unfortunately it is not often that the relations of the sick person will allow one to do so. To win over the mother was, as usual, the principal thing; I thought I had detected an expression of anxious confidence in her eyes each time she looked at me, on the strength of which I ventured to make the attempt—if anything was to be done it was necessary to set about it at once; the rubbing had proved useless, and the child was sinking fast. Whilst I was preparing my instruments (out here, like surgeons in time of war, one is obliged to make the best of everything and content oneself with very little) a heated discussion arose in the room, resulting in very divided opinions, most of the women voting in favour of "*lasciare fare la Madonna*,"[1] and the whole thing being brought to a conclusion by the mother's cry : "*Sia fatto la volontà di Dio e di San Gennaro Benedetto!*"[2]—whereupon I was allowed to

[1] "Let the Blessed Virgin do as she likes."
[2] "May the will of God and of Blessed St. Gennaro be done."

proceed. But hardly had I made the incision and exposed the vein than they all shrieked aloud, and as the child, to my horror, collapsed a moment afterwards, the mother cried in her despair, "*Mi muore, mi muore !*"[1]

Just then one of the women pointed to the Blessed Virgin's image, and speechless with terror, they saw *la lampada* flicker and go out. A dead silence fell over the room, and then all of them dropped on their knees and crossed themselves repeatedly; the old grandmother alone moved neither hand nor foot; seated in her dark corner she continued to shake her head and mutter : "*Ira di Dio, ira di Dio!*"[2] The mother darted towards the image, and seizing it with both hands, cried aloud in a tone of voice that was almost threatening, "*Perchè ai fatto spegnere la lampada, Madonna Santa? Vorresti far spegnere così la vita della piccola?*

[1] " She is dying, she is dying !"
  " The wrath of God, the wrath of God ! "

E tu fai grazie? E tu sei madre del Dio? No, no, non avresti cuore, non avresti viscere di madre. . . ." [1]

She poured fresh oil into the lamp and placed two lighted candles before the little statue : *"ora te ne ò portato due ceri benedetti—va bene così? Tu sei contenta adesso, Madonna mia ?"* [2]

I sat there with the inanimate child in my arms, fully alive to the savage and suspicious eyes that were following my slightest movements.

I shall not forget that night in a hurry.

They had interpreted the extinction of the sacred lamp as a death-warrant, and therefore none of them had even attempted to come to my assistance. Amidst alternate prayers addressed to the Ma-

---

[1] "Why didst thou extinguish the lamp, O Holy Virgin? Is it thus that thou wouldst extinguish the life of my little one? And thou art full of grace ! And thou art the Mother of God? No, no, thou hast not the heart, the bowels of a mother."

[2] "Now have I brought thee two votive candles—is all well now? Art thou satisfied now, O Holy Virgin?"

donna and threats hurled at myself, the night wore on. I expected the child to die every moment, and began at last to ask myself, whether, in point of fact, it was not my own life that I was watching over. There I sat, gazing fixedly at the child, wiping the cold perspiration off her forehead and off my own ; I had done everything that lay in my power, and had given up all hope. At last the cold, gray daylight fell into the room, and upon a corpse, as I should have thought, but for the fact that I was still able to distinguish the faint beating of her heart.

Towards morning a sort of reaction set in, the heart-beats became steadier, the pulse appreciable, and to some slight degree the warmth of life returned. Again she began to moan, and you should have seen the mother's face as the child's voice fell upon her ear : " *Mammà, mammà !* "

I was wrong again, thank God—the child was returning to life.

I left the house shortly afterwards,

followed by the father, and after threading our way through a labyrinth of lanes and alleys we emerged on to the Piazza Mercato. I gave him his instructions for the day, and he gazed at me with an expression that more than compensated for the sleepless night. According to our agreement we met again that night, and I was happy indeed to hear his first words : "*Sta meglior, sia benedetto San Gennaro!*" [1]

Yes ! she really was better, and after I had been to see her the next evening, I ventured to hope that her recovery was assured. I saw her three days running, being each time accompanied there and back by the father, who always met me on the Piazza Mercato. I no longer insisted on going there alone and by daylight, for I had discovered that they very much preferred to receive my visits after dark. The evening of my last visit I was on terms of the firmest friendship with the whole lot—always excepting the old crone,

[1] "She is better, blessed be St. Gennaro !"

who sat there muttering, "*Ammazzacane*"[1] at me the whole time—and as I left the house towards night time, the mother stood upon the doorstep, and watched me down the street, and long did her last words ring in my ears: "*Possiate avere la pace che desiderate !*"[2] Poor woman, she was wishing me what seemed to her the best and most desirable of all things, and it was no fault of hers that she happened to wish me the one good thing that never can be mine !

As I took leave of the father I asked him what his name was, and he answered, "Salvatore Trapanese"—it did not interest me as a doctor, but the family initials were certainly not those that stood engraved upon the silver cup into which I had poured the child's medicine.

Don Salvatore added that if ever I wanted him, his services, his life, and his

[1] "Dog's murderer"; one of the usual epithets applied by the people to the Medical Staff.

[2] "May the peace which you desire be granted unto you !"

coltello [1] were at my disposal. He then pointed in the direction of the Via Lavinaio, where a ragged old *ciabattino* [2] (*sole-chianiello*, as the people say) was seated cobbling a pair of boots, and told me that if ever I required anything I had only to address myself to him.

I thanked him for his kindness, and he in his ignorance thanked me for his child's life, and then we bade each other farewell.

* *

*

This was not much of a story, neither was it, for the matter of that, the one I meant to tell you at the outset. I often went down to that part of the town, but never came across Don Salvatore again, and ere long had completely forgotten the whole affair.

But I heard on all sides that the insecurity in the poor quarters was very great during the whole of that period ; the

---

[1] Knife.   [2] Cobbler.

newspapers teemed with accounts, more or less gruesome, of nightly attacks, whilst the Camorra appeared to be displaying an amount of vitality unexampled since the good old days when half Naples was under the sway of this extraordinary institution.

Personally, I had never been exposed to the slightest danger, in fact I began to wonder whether a good many of these descriptions were not all moonshine. One evening, however, whilst wandering through the Vicaria quarter, I fancied that I was being followed by a very suspicious-looking character. I had something to attend to up in that direction, and am bound to admit that, after having had the fellow at my heels for so long, I experienced a certain amount of relief upon reaching the Fondaco, where I had plenty of good friends. The man to whom my visit was intended had died in the meantime, so that I did not remain there more than a few minutes.

By the time I left the house it had be-

come quite dark, and hardly had I got under
way before I heard stealthy footsteps in the
rear. The rule to be followed on these
sort of occasions is a very simple one, all
one has to do is to keep one's back free.
I therefore pulled up once or twice to allow
the night-walker to get ahead, but each
time I did so the sound of his footsteps
died suddenly away, and had I not, every
now and again, detected a dark shadow
upon the wall, I would most assuredly have
concluded that what I heard was nothing
further than the echo of my own footsteps.
But Puck growled suspiciously the whole
time, and as I crossed the Piazzetta dei
S. S. Apostoli I discovered my pursuer
and the man who had dogged my footsteps the whole evening, to be one and the
same person. I turned a minute afterwards into the Via del Duomo, the only
decent street in the quarter, where a certain amount of traffic goes on all night.
I stood for ever so long at the corner
just to see whether he would follow me

up, but the blackguard was afraid to show himself in the well-lit street. The next evening I was again followed at some little distance by the same rascal. I went the whole way home on foot, but after reaching my room, happened to step out on to the balcony for a moment, and there he was, sure enough, still hanging about the street corner. He lingered there for a little while—but was frustrated for the second time, as I had no intention of going out again that evening.

That the fellow in question had some sort of design upon me I was no longer able to doubt, for wherever I went he would suddenly make his appearance, and I could easily see, notwithstanding all his efforts, that he did his best to hide his espionage from me. One night I actually found him standing outside the cholera cemetery—the burials always took place at midnight, so that I did not get away till the small hours.

But for the matter of that I never saw

him until after dark—like all beasts of prey he lay concealed during the day.

One gets used to everything in time, and very likely I should have become quite accustomed to having this man at my heels—in spite of his uncanny appearance—but for the fact that my misgivings received ere long a direct confirmation that left nothing to be desired in the way of intelligibility.

I stood one evening upon the Molo, gazing at the twilight as it spread over the bay, whilst high up against the darkening firmament I saw old Vesuvius light the lights in his gigantic watch-tower.

All of a sudden I saw my man dash up to the pier, jump into a boat, and row out to sea in a desperate hurry. The next moment two "*carabinieri*" jumped into another boat and began to pursue him. In less than one minute at least a hundred people had assembled on the beach, all of them watching the race with breathless interest, and one enthusiastic urchin who stood beside me, shouting: "*coraggio, coraggio!*" after the fugitive, informed me that the man whom they were trying to catch was a Camorrist. The bay was swarming with fishing-smacks returning from their day's work, and it was easy to see that they did their best to get in the way of the carabineers' boat. One of the carabineers drew his revolver, but hardly had the first report resounded than the Camorrist threw himself into the sea. It was so dark that I was unable to see anything, but the others assured me that he was unhurt, and could still be seen swimming in the direction of a large boat that had just hoisted her sails to go out fishing for the night. She made straight for the swimmer, and for a moment it seemed as though he really would succeed in reaching her—in which case he would be perfectly safe, as the pursuers had no sail, and once it was dark it would be easy enough to land him somewhere on the coast. (I have sailed in a smuggler's boat myself, and know for a fact that coastguards are but few and far between).

The people by whom I was surrounded made no secret of their sympathy for the Camorrist, and I was surprised to find myself hoping that he would get off——I know this sounds very bad, but I can't help that, it isn't often that I side with the police, at all events in this part of the world.

Justice, however, carried the day this time, they managed to secure him, and a moment afterwards landed with their prisoner. His hands were tied behind him, and he was so exhausted by his long struggle that he could hardly drag himself along between the two carabineers.

Most of the crowd followed him down the much-dreaded road to the San Francesco prison. But I stood there for ever so long, rooted to the ground, as it were, for as he had passed me, the prisoner had raised his head, and his eyes had dwelt upon my face with an extraordinary ex-

P

pression, in which hatred and reproach were strangely mingled.

The next day I read in the *Pungolo* newspaper that a dangerous Camorrist had been arrested on the Molo after a desperate struggle, the police being of opinion that they were at last on the track of a gang of Camorrists guilty of every sort of outrage.

My practice had become quite large in the people's quarter, and it was there that I spent the greater part of the day, more especially in the Mercato and Porto districts. Experience had taught me how to deal with these poor people, and I had managed to secure several good friends for myself amongst them. And just about this time it seemed to me that the circle of my acquaintance began to augment very considerably. Wherever I went, first one ragamuffin and then another would nod to me, and on my way home at night, friendly greetings of "*Buona sera, Eccellenza !*" were bestowed upon me by night-wanderers with whom, to the best of my belief, I had no acquaintance whatsoever. The cabmen on the Piazza Mercato began to crack their whips as soon as they caught sight of me, shouting after me in a tone of voice very unlike their usual one, " *Signò, vulìt a mme !* " and did I not care to drive, they were none the less friendly on that account.

Did I enter some little *osteria* or *bottegha* I noticed more than once that a nod exchanged between the guests and the host resulted in a double amount of attention towards myself, and once that I had already settled down to my *fiaschetto* of wine the innkeeper came up and exchanged it for a bottle of good *vino vecchio*, but not before I had detected an animated series of gesticulations between himself and the driver who sat outside waiting for me.

Of course I was flattered by all this attention, but could not help wondering at the extraordinary development of my friendly relations. What puzzled me most of all, however, was the fact that another fellow had begun to follow me about wherever I went, and once or twice he followed me up to my own door. He was quite as suspicious-looking as his predecessor, and it soon became quite evident that he had completely taken upon himself the other man's inexplicable *rôle* of nightly espionage.

One day I was driven down to the Porta Capuana by a cabman who overwhelmed me with attentions, though I did not recollect having ever seen him before. We drove past the San Francesco prison, and just as we passed the gate the driver winked mysteriously at me, and the following conversation ensued—I think I had better translate the Neapolitan dialect in which it took place, as you would certainly be unable to make it out :—

" Has Eccellenza been to see him ? " said the driver.

" Whom ? "

"Is not Eccellenza aware that he was arrested and put into prison?   But it was his own fault, what business had he to show himself on the Molo, where he was sure to come across a policeman?   And Eccellenza is in no way to blame."

"But, *sapristi*, whom are you talking about?"

"*Il fratello del vostro amico*"[1] said the driver, winking for the second time.

It was Don Salvatore's brother who had been arrested on the Molo.

*   *

*

My expeditions came to an untimely end the very next day, for I fell ill myself—Naples is such an unhealthy place, you know.   It wasn't much to speak of, but still it came upon me very suddenly. I believe I fainted in the street, for when at last I rubbed my eyes and looked about me, I found myself half-lying in a

[1] "The brother of our friend.

cab and seated opposite a policeman, who, pale as death, was staring at me with an expression of absolute terror in his face. I tried to recall what had gone before, and wondered what sort of a crime it could be for which I had been arrested, but my head was altogether too weak, and as for the Camorra, Don Salvatore, my-self, and the San Francesco prison, I had muddled them all up together.

" *Sta un poco meglio?* " [1] said the police-man.

"*Gnorsì* " [2] (= *sì*), I answered, in genuine Neapolitan dialect.

"*Coraggio, un altro poco siamo arri-vato!* " [3] were his next words.

We drove down the Strada Piliero, and the sea-breeze blew over my forehead, where by slow degrees everything seemed to become clearer and clearer. Suddenly I remembered the fact that I was a doc-tor, and begged the policeman to put his

[1] "Do you feel better?"   [2] "Yes."
[3] "Courage! another moment, and we shall be there."

hand in my pocket and give me the bottle of ether which he would find there, but, by the way he touched my coat, you would have thought I had asked him to put his hand into a fiery furnace.

Every now and again the people in the street turned round to look at us, and I noticed that they made the sign of the cross as we drove past.

We were on our way to the Santa Maddalena cholera hospital.

By this time I had become capable of thinking tolerably well again, and had come to the conclusion that the Santa Maddalena hospital was an uncanny sort of place, after all; the policeman, I discovered, was entirely of my opinion, whereupon at my request we drew up before a little public-house, where, in a bumper of pretty stiff cognac, I drank his health, whilst he and the driver each tossed off their own *foglietta* of wine.

I told the policeman I required no doctor, that I was in fact a doctor my-

self, and quite convinced in my own mind
that this was no attack of cholera; and
the kind-hearted fellow told me that that
was just what he had thought all along—
"*un poco di febbre*,"[1] that was all.

I got home right enough, but remember
nothing after reaching the door. Immediately after my arrival I found that
Cæsare was dropping bits of ice into my
mouth, and as I opened my eyes I noticed
that the evening sun was still streaming
into the room; but Cæsare said it wasn't
the same sun—I had been lying there for
twenty-four hours, so he informed me.

Having skipped the whole of that time
in my own mind I think I may just as
well do so here. I asked Cæsare—
Cæsare was my servant, groom of the
chambers, cook, anything you like—if I
was down with the cholera, but I did not
recognise my own voice, which sounded
like that of an infirm old woman. Cæsare
answered that he was not quite sure, but

---

[1] "A little fever."

that on the whole he feared it was so—his opinion was not without a certain weight, for he had seen his own wife and child die of the same disease.

Yes, it was very possible that it was cholera, although the symptoms did not strike me as the usual ones, but cholera was never absent from one's mind during those days, and I felt curious to see what the night would bring forth.

Cæsare had gone out—to get more ice, so he said—and I lay pondering there alone.

When one's head is weak, one's thoughts are always sad, and at last *one tries to give up thinking altogether.* One feels so tired that one longs to lie down and rest in peace for good and all. To die is not so terrible, but cowardly natures shrink from the idea of a lengthened period of suffering.

It is a psychological error to suppose that familiarity with the death-struggles of our fellow-creatures is apt to breed more confidence in us when face to face with death ourselves ; it may be true as far as others are concerned, but when after calm and dispassionate reflection, one is more or less convinced that the last hours of one's own life are at hand, one begins to wish that one had never seen what it is to die. "Be a man," one says to oneself, "and if you have not known how to live, show at least that you know how to die!"

Yet ceaselessly does one's imagination conjure up visions of the terrified eyes that have so often sought for hope in the expression of one's own, when, as doctor, one has stood beside the deathbed ; again and again there rings in one's ears the hoarse cry for help even after all power of speech and thought has fled, again one looks upon the stiffening fingers that one has so often seen grasping spasmodically at the bedclothes, even as a drowning man grasps at a straw, and groping feverishly in search of some hand whereon to cling to life, again and again one calls to mind the gasping breast, which, straining

every muscle to catch a breath of air,
strives, for one or two brief moments more,
to prolong the struggle with the execu-
tioner, who slowly but surely continues
to strangle his victim. Yes, Heine was
right: "*Der Tod ist nichts, aber das Sterben
ist eine schändliche Erfindung !*"[1]

The window stood wide open, and I
could see right away across the bay.
Everything looked so bright and happy
outside, it seemed to me the shores had
decked themselves more radiantly than
ever to bid me farewell. I looked out on
to Capri, which lay there wrapped in
roseate slumber, and I could not help
thinking that it would be very hard should
I indeed be obliged to say good-bye for
ever to the place I loved so well. A sort
of mist fell over the bay, and I heard
voices from the joys of my life calling me
by my name.

And then there was a dead silence ; it

[1] "Death is nothing, but dying is an ignominious
invention."

became quite dark, and a feeling of utter loneliness came over me.

I stretched my hand out to my friend, but he sat not beside me; I called him by his name, but he did not come. I tried to think he had only gone out with Cæsare and breathlessly I began to listen for the sound of his footstep on the stairs. Presently the door was quietly opened, and Cæsare entered on tip-toe. " Where is he ? " I asked. Cæsare evaded the question, assuring me that he would be back in a moment; but I insisted on hearing the whole truth, and then I realised that I was alone—quite alone.

Cæsare had happened to be looking out of the window at the time of my arrival, and had carried me upstairs, for I had fainted in the endeavour to get out of the carriage. The driver had seen nothing of Puck, and Cæsare had been so horrified at my appearance that, sorry as I am to have to confess it, he had never even attempted to find out what had become

of him till a few moments ago, when he
had rushed downstairs to send for the
consul, and I am not quite sure that
even then it was entirely on Puck's account
that he took these steps.   I did my best
to lash myself into a rage with him, but
felt so tired that I was obliged to give it up.

The consul turned up almost immediately.   He was a good fellow, but had
no notion what the matter was, having
misunderstood the whole affair from beginning to end ; however, once he had
realised the situation, he promised to do
all that lay in his power to find Puck.
He then said he hoped his endeavours on
his behalf would be more successful than
those he had made on mine.   He had a
heap of letters and telegrams for me, and
had himself received a telegram some time
ago directing him to try and find out
whether I were "dead or alive" ; he had
done his best to do so, but the Authorities
had been unable to tell him anything
about me.

I laughed in my sleeve, sad as I felt, and asked him if he did not think it would be just as well to wait for a day or two before answering that telegram. Cæsare followed him downstairs, and I heard my factotum volunteer this piece of information to the consul in the course of their whispered conversation : "*Parla con lo cane come era un Cristiano.*" [1]

Towards evening I received a line from the consul to the effect that a hue and cry had been raised on Puck's account; that every policeman in Naples had received orders to be on the look-out, and that I had every reason to hope for the best.

My sickness did not develop into real cholera, and there I lay the whole night through, waiting for some of the well-known symptoms to declare themselves, but they did not make their appearance after all. I felt rather better next day,

[1] "He speaks to the dog as though he were a Christian."

but far too restless to bother about myself, as you may well imagine.

But perhaps having got thus far you are laughing at my expense—well, if that's the case, all I can say is, you are welcome to laugh as much as you like! But I found it no laughing matter, I can tell you, as I lay there thinking of the faithful friend I had lost.

I recollected how for eight whole years we had fought the battle of life together, how for eight whole years we had stuck to one another through thick and thin, honestly sharing the heavy burdens and the light. I recollected how when I was happy he was happy too, never once stopping to think whether he himself had any grounds for rejoicing, he asked no questions, to share my pleasure was all he cared about—a look, a nod, a friendly word, and his honest face would light up with the gladness that he saw in mine.

And were I depressed and low-spirited he would sit beside me, just as miserable himself. He never tried to cheer me up, for he was well aware of the insufficiency of consolatory words, he said nothing, for he knew that silence is soothing when one is feeling sad. But steadily would he look at me and softly lay his head upon my knee. He knew that his poor brain was unable to keep pace with mine, but still his faithful heart claimed his share of my grief.

Did others vote me rough and cross-grained, his patient forbearance would overlook it all, and his friendship stand proof against every injustice. And were I irritable and hard upon him when I left the house, yet did he always return good for evil, and affectionately and good-humouredly would he always run to greet me when I came back.

Others might sit in judgment on my many faults, and abuse me up hill and down dale, but eagerly and lovingly he always strove to look at everything from the least unfavourable point of view, refusing to believe that I was capable of wrong. Did I enter heart and soul into some cause or other, defending it to the best of my abilities, the rest of the world might abuse me for my pains, but he was always of the same opinion as myself. And in the hour of need, when other friends were not forthcoming, he always stood beside me, ready to shield me from every danger, and glad, if need be, to lay his life down for my sake.

We had seen a good deal of the world, we two, we had come across a good many specimens of humanity, our experience of life was large enough. We were ambitious once upon a time, ay, that we were—very ambitious indeed. Both of us dreamed dreams about first prizes and honourable mentions, dreams in which the finest Persian carpets lay beneath our feet, and dreams in which savoury little birds, all ready cooked, flew into our mouths. That time is over, and one of us is already gray, but no savoury little birds have flown into our mouths as yet,

Q

and no Persian carpets have made their appearance either, for the matter of that. And if the floor be damp and cold I spread my own coat for my faithful comrade.

Once upon a time we had a very good opinion of mankind. We were idealists because we thought the rest of the world were idealists too. We were tender-hearted and kind because we thought that others were the same. We were philanthropists.

But after a while we found out how mistaken we were, and came to the conclusion that there was not much love lost between most of our fellow-creatures. They talked a good deal about friendship, but we found out how few of them had any conception of the word's significance and depth.

And one and all they laughed me to scorn because I dignified a dog's unselfish devotion by the name of friendship, because gratefully I strove to repay, as far as lay in my power, the humble comrade

of my life who according to their lights
was nothing but a soulless animal, whose
keen and sensitive understanding they
dismissed as mere instinct, and whose
honest, upright soul, they said, would live
no longer than his faithful heart!

If his all-sacrificing, all-charitable affec-
tion be not *virtue*, well, then I do not
know what virtue means—and if he is
merely to be shot in his old age and
buried beneath some tree in the park
at home, if that is the only reward that
is to be meted out to him in return for
his life's devotion—well, then all that I
can say is, I don't believe that any of us
either will ever get beyond the graves in
which we shall be laid some day!

And where was he now, my faithful
friend? Fallen perhaps into the hands
of some hard-hearted brute who was
kicking and ill-treating him, for aught
I knew, sitting there bound fast and
anxiously waiting for me to come to the
rescue—and I—incapable of putting one

leg before the other. I had an idea that were I only able to get out myself I should find him in less than no time, and all but cried over my utter helplessness. I begged and prayed Cæsare to help me into my clothes, I stormed at him, hoping thereby to induce him to carry me down to a cab, but he turned a deaf ear to all my entreaties. The consul came to see me that same evening, but brought no tidings of the dog, and then I made up my mind that he was lost to me for ever. He did his best to cheer me up, and told me that a friend of his had lost his dog twice, in precisely the same way, but that he had recovered him on both occasions, and that he now paid a Camorrist five francs a year to see that the dog was left alone.

After the consul had left, Cæsare and I held a council of war. Neither of us reposed much confidence in the Municipal Authorities, and Cæsare's antipathy to the police was, if anything, more pronounced

than mine. That same evening Cæsare
went down to the Piazza Mercato to hunt
up the old *ciabattino*, and about eleven
o'clock an individual made his appearance,
whom, under any other circumstances, I
should have been startled to see in my
room at that time of night. He greeted
me in a familiar sort of way, and asked
me if I recognised him, but I was obliged
to confess I didn't. He looked like the
devil himself. He was the bearer of
greetings from Don Salvatore who, on
account of important engagements, was
unable to come himself, but he begged me
to rest assured that he was my very good
friend. I thanked him for his kind ex-
pressions, and told him all about Puck.
I took up my purse, emptied its contents
on to the bed, and told him that everything I possessed should be handed over
to whosoever brought the dog back. The
state of my finances is never very brilliant,
I don't believe I had more than 200
francs in the house. He listened atten-

tively, and I shall never forget his words as I ceased speaking: "*Si non è morto sara ççà domani sera !*" [1]

I asked him if he felt quite sure of himself, and told him that I knew what cunning fellows those dog-stealers were, but as he answered with a certain amount of dignity, "*Sono tutti miei amici*," [2] I felt that I had underrated his influence.

I thanked him for the hopes he had given me, and then he left me. He turned as he reached the door and invoked the protection of the Blessed Virgin and San Gennaro on my behalf. And then I recognised him—he was the man who had followed me ever since the first one had been arrested on the Molo.

I slept better that night, and next morning it was quite evident that the consul might telegraph that I was still alive, with perfect truth, and without any

[1] "You shall have him back to-morrow evening, if he be not dead !"

[2] "They are all friends of mine."

danger of being put to the expense of contradicting the news. But as the day wore on I grew more and more restless. There I lay worrying myself more than ever, having suddenly recollected that the day before I fell ill I had been rather hard on—not to say downright unjust— to poor Puck, and you cannot think how unceasingly this thought recurred to me, and how wretched it made me feel.

And evening came, and yet no news. Cæsare had been told to stand on watch down below in the street, and now that he again saw fit to obey my orders he had actually gone and left me alone for a few moments. I was so tired after all this worry that at last I fell into a sort of half-sleep. I don't know how long I lay there in the dark, but I know how I was awoken. Cæsare came rushing into the room, I heard a panting on the stairs that very nearly caused me to try and jump out of bed, and Puck dashed into the room, dragging Don Salvatore after him. Don

Salvatore let go of him, and my dear old dog came bounding up to the bed and laid his great head softly on my breast. His bonny coat was torn and bloody, and round his neck there hung a great thick piece of rope.

Neither of us said a word—neither he nor I, but we have never stood in need of words to understand each other.

Don Salvatore stood quietly in the doorway. He looked pale and tired, and was about as ragged as my friend of the day before, but notwithstanding the soiled and torn condition of his coat, the white band upon the sleeve was visible.[1]

I reached him my hand and thanked him for the happiness he had procured

[1] When a child falls ill, the parents invariably make a vow to the Blessed Virgin for its recovery. They promise to wear her colours for a certain period, sometimes for years, and nothing in the world would induce them to lay them aside before the expiration of the time. Brown, with a binding of white, is what is worn in honour of the Madonna del Carmine, white with red bindings for the Madonna delle Salette, etc.

me, but he looked almost confused, and I noticed that he tried to avoid my eye: "*Sono un uomo di mala vita*," said he; "*e non sono degno di toccar la vostra mano.*"[1]

I had certainly no reason for being hard on any one, but I had several excellent reasons for being hard on no one; and so I told him.

And then I handed him the money, but he put it back on to the table with these words: "*Voi avete salvato la figliuola, io ho trovato lo cane—va bene così!*"[2]

And then he threw his ragged cloak over his shoulder and took himself off.

But I think I owe Don Salvatore even more than the recovery of my dog!

[1] "I am a bad man, and not worthy of touching your hand."

[2] "You saved the little girl, I found the dog—it is all right now!"

XIV

GOLFO DI NAPOLI

 STOOD the other day upon the Immacolatella, and beside me stood Rosina, buried deep in thought. How we came to be there is more than I can say—but somehow or other we had drifted thither.

The Immacolatella is the harbour for all the fishing-boats upon the bay, but now that Naples is inaccessible from the sea, the place is absolutely empty.

"*Un bajocco, Signoria! Eccellenza! un bajocco!*"

Ah yes! we are so familiarised with that appeal by now that I instantly pretend not to have heard it. But the beggar was not to be put off—he must be a bit of a psychologist, thought I, as I put my hand into my pocket with the intention of handing him over his percentage on the *Dagblad* letters, poor ragged fellow, his right to a share of the proceeds is certainly greater than mine.

" *Pietà, Signoria !* " There was a ring of such despair in the tone of the man's voice, that I instantly made up my mind to deal him out a sort of extra field-service allowance, and then take myself off as quickly as possible—I felt quite sure that it was hunger and destitution that had blanched the lips that were appealing to my charity at that very moment, and could not trust myself to look at him, knowing that if I did so, a whole column of the *Dagblad* would disappear into his pocket, and economy was the order of the day in those hard times.

I spurred Rosina on . . . that is to say, I suggested that we should go and

see what the bay was like a little
lower down. Fate, however, had decreed
that just then she should be wholly ab-
sorbed in the solution of some vexed
problem, and not an inch did we stir off
the spot—I have already confided to you
elsewhere how much I respect liberty of
thought ; besides, there was no other alter-
native, for, as you may perhaps remember,
Kant's philosophy, according to Rosina,
is open to a good deal of criticism, and
she has always refused point-blank to
admit his *Kategorische Imperativ*.

The beggar was still standing there
with the coppers I had given him in his
hand, when suddenly I happened to look
the ragged fellow straight in the face—
Sapristi ! it was Francesco himself, the
very same Francesco who was with me
five years ago, one stormy autumn evening that we were driven into Pola, and it was
under his own cloak that, frozen and wet,
I slept the whole night through ! Povero
Francesco, what is the meaning of this ?

And Francesco, quite as astonished as myself at coming across a friend upon the Immacolatella, welcomed me with an outburst of genuine Southern eloquence— the big fellow fairly sobbed as he told me that two months had already elapsed since his return from coral-fishing in " Barbaria," (Algiers), two months which he had spent on shore waiting in vain for permission to land at Capri.

He had not been able to find work, his savings had come to an end, and to-day he had been obliged to beg his bread.

I put Francesco up that night—when one has lain for weeks together under a boat, one's ideas of comfort are not apt to be extensive, and it was Francesco this time who slept under the cover of my cloak.

The rest of his unfortunate companions, so he told me, had lingered in Sorrento, waiting for permission to return home.

Regular communication between Sorrento and Naples had only just been reestablished, and next morning we both went over in the steamboat. We had hardly reached the Marina before I recognised a host of old Capriot acquaintances, and I was distressed indeed to see the misery to which they were reduced.

During the first few weeks they had received five soldi a day from Capri, but after a while this assistance had been withdrawn, Sorrento found that it was as much as she could do to succour her own distressed inhabitants, and the poor devils were now living on the charity of their Sorrentinian companions down on the Marina. Most of them were coral fishermen from Africa, a few others were sailors on their way home after a prolonged absence, and the rest were simple fishermen who had been out fishing in the open sea. Twice already had they sailed over to Capri endeavouring to land, and during their last attempt the quarantine officials had threatened to fire on their boat. We held a meeting down on the Marina that

same afternoon, for the express purpose
of talking the matter over and deciding
what was to be done ; our speeches were
neither lengthy nor brilliant, but we were
all of one mind, which was the principal
thing, all agreeing that the best thing to
do was to make one more attempt, and
set off the next morning.

Before the commencement of our meeting I had hastily run over to greet
Donna Mariucci, the friendly hostess of
the little osteria, which in former days
it had been my custom to frequent. And
whilst our cogitations were going on
below, the maccaroni was steaming away
above in the padrona's largest saucepan,
and shortly afterwards the whole of the
Capriot colony was seated round the
dining-table in the garden below.

A rare feast, my friend, this feast of ours
beneath the shadows of the orange-trees,
the sun setting in a blaze of glory behind
us, the murmur of the waves beneath us,
the rich ripe grapes, the brilliant blue

figs, and the golden oranges above us!
You, who have never tasted anything
but the adulterated, sour wines they give
you in the hotels, you should have had
a draught of some of Donna Mariucci's
rich old wine, pressed from the purest
grapes, in the same simple way that was
the custom of the land 2000 years ago,
innocent of all modern ingredients, fragrant as the flowers, joyous as the summer's
sun! The wine is old, my friend—it is
the same wine that Horace drank with
the song upon his lips, and the bays upon
his brow!

Sorrento is not much of a place, the
news of our banquet has run swiftly
down to its only harbour upon the naked
feet of many a little urchin, and one by
one the fishermen's bonnets make their
appearance above the garden wall.

Welcome, all good friends, here is a
glass of prime old wine in which you
can drink to our *buon viaggio* to-morrow morning! A good many of these

Sorrentinians are old acquaintances of mine—types of honest, friendly, sunburnt fishermen, every one of them. The introduction to the newcomers is accomplished by general desire without any disturbing element of etiquette.

" *Chi è* " ? I hear them ask one after the other, pointing towards me. And with a look of the profoundest importance and mystery, his Capriot neighbour whispers into his ear : " *E il Signor con lo cane.*" [1] " *Il Signor con lo cane !* " — Ah well, that name is just as good as any other, once upon a time it belonged to a very happy fellow, and I am very proud of the title. [2] And to-day is a grand day for me, it is such a joy to see how well these good, kind people have remembered me, and it is not the generous old wine, ah no, it is the blind love with which I worship the

[1] The gentleman with the dog.

[2] Puck has often been here ; his last " villegiatura " in Capri extended over a year. He is the biggest dog in Southern Italy, and enjoys a widespread and deserved popularity.

R

country itself, that fills me, heart and soul, with such a sense of jubilant gladness.

And here comes Narella, the padrona's youngest daughter, to inquire if "il Signor" still remembers that they have danced the tarantella together on more than one occasion. Ay, Narella mia, I remember it well enough, and bring hither the tambourin and guitar, to-day, when I would take the whole world to my arms, thou mayest be sure I'll dance the tarantella right willingly with the prettiest girl in all Sorrento !

And whilst the young ones dance upon the terrace down below, the old men smoke their pipes above, glancing from time to time towards the bay, and wondering from which quarter the wind will blow on the morrow.

At last we separate to meet again next day on the Marina, where the boat lies ready and waiting for us.

And thank ye for this day *tutti quanti !*

and thank ye for your kindly remembrance of me during the past years!

"*Grazia a voi Signorì!*"—Nay, do not thank me, thank the *Dagblad;* we have dined off the "*two Pessimists*," and eaten up the whole article from beginning to end!

And now the twilight falls across Sorrento's mountains, the murmur of the sea grows fainter and fainter, the bells ring out the Angelus,—good-night!

*   *

*

A Sorrentinian summer's day, my friend!

The sun stands high above Monte St. Angelo, and darts his brilliant rays upon the glittering blue of the gulf beneath. Still dreaming in the west lies Ischia, enveloped in the roseate mist of early dawn, whilst Posilipo drapes herself in green and glorious raiment. Naples awakes in purple and gold, whilst Portici,

Resina, and Torre del Greco cast their glittering string of pearls about the foot of Vesuvius. There lies the volcano in gigantic repose; summer has flung her verdant mantle about his loins, but has not dared to venture higher up,—the sun alone is allowed to approach the summit, and strew his gold upon the Titan's gray head. A little cloud, the offspring of the youthful day, is gazing boldly into the giant's very jaws, but he is slumbering still, and the vapour of each deep-drawn breath stands out against the clear blue sky. Other clouds come sailing from afar, floating out over the dark violet-tinted mountains to the gulf beyond. They are going in the same direction as ourselves, high overhead they sail along in all their pride, and down below we spread our sails upon Sorrento's shores, but the same blue light is irradiating heaven and earth, and the same soft wind is directing our onward course.

The sails are swelling in the morning

breeze, and with seething foam at the bow, the port gunwale tearing through the water, and the ripple of the waves under the keel, we bid farewell to Sorrento.

Off with thy hat and let the wind blow straight across thy brow! Unbutton thy coat and inhale the splendid air in long deep draughts, for it is pure and sweet as early spring, and fresh as Nature's youth itself! Long enough hast thou dwelt in the city's stifling atmosphere, long enough hast thou wandered through its dusty streets and infected sickrooms, long enough have sorrow and misery cast their gloomy shadows over thee—now let boundless space stretch forth its health-restoring arms to thee, now let the sea flow out to meet thee, and to flood thee with its buoyant gladness!

Look up at thy fellow-travellers overhead, look up at the clouds that but a moment ago shut out the sun from view, hath not the wind driven them far away? are not the heavens clear again—and shall

not the fresh sea-breeze likewise drive
away the sorrow that hath dimmed the
gladness of thy spirit for so long! Look
out upon the bay into which Naples pours
her refuse, yet see how glitteringly blue it
is—shall not its sparkling waters purify
thee also from the dust-stains of the
shore!

Oh, how doth now thy breast expand,
dost thou not feel the winds of heaven
blowing into the innermost depths of thy
soul, spreading the sails for many a
youthful thought that hath lain at anchor
for so long! Thou hearest how thy
heart is throbbing in even, steady beats,
even as a pendulum, it is the mid-day of
thy life, full well thou knowest that the
works within are strong and good—and
now they'll go again for many a day to
come, 'twas but the mainspring that was
out of order!

The wind is rising, and the boat dances
merrily over the rolling waves. Let the
salt sea spray dash over thy face, it is

better than the richest wine, it is the
frothy, sparkling mother's milk that, flowing from the undulating bosom of Nature,
shall win thee back to health and strength!

Thou who hast dared to doubt that
miracles exist, now do the scales fall from
thine eyes, and thou seest that the world
is beautiful still, beautiful as on Creation's
day. Oh, how great a light has risen up
within thee! The spectre of thy sickly
hypochondria vanishes into space, and
broken-winged and dazzled by the light,
Minerva's owl flies round the barren
walls of thy philosophy's pessimistic pagan
temple. And presently the ruins of thy
proud seat of learning sink to the bottom
of the sea, and the glad waves dance joy-
ously over the bitter human thoughts,
and deep down below, the pearls and
corals grow over thy barren philosophies
and cynical theories. Thy sages go to
the bottom with the philosophers' stone
round their neck, and down in his ocean
halls below, sits Neptune, stroking his

white beard, and laughing so heartily at
the forlorn appearance of the new arrivals,
that the very waves on the surface grow
frothier, and the mermaids snatch at the
poor professors' wigs, whilst the fish dart
merrily in and out the holes of their
philosophers' mantles.

But thou who sittest in thy boat above,
thou dost not dare to breathe another
word of rebellious suffering, mutely thou
gazest into the blue immensity above, from
whence the sun, as from a temple's arched
vault, doth proclaim his radiant philosophy,
and grateful and humble thou stretchest
forth thine arms to life again !

The coast along which we sail is so
beautiful that one almost wishes the
wind would drop, to enable one to enjoy
the beauty of the scene a little longer.

There you can see Capo di Sorrento, and
the walls upon the rock over there date
from the time of the Romans ; the people
call them "Bagno della Regina Giovanna,"
but they are really the ruins of an

antique bath. The columns beside it
are the remains of a temple dedicated—
some say to Hercules, others to Neptune.
I myself believe that it was the sea-god
who used to dwell here, and can you not
tell by the rapidity of our course "how
Father Neptune himself, with his mighty
hand, doth push the boat on as she
moves"?[1] Old Virgil is the right man
to quote here, for he has so often sailed
across this very bay, and spread the same
latin sail against the wind as we ourselves. And it is along these very coasts
that Æneas wandered, and on the promontory yonder did Ulysses raise a temple
to Minerva. The place now goes by the
name of Punta di Campanella ; everything about here is so old that to you
there is a modern ring about the name
—it only dates from the time of Charles
the Fifth, and from here it is that they

---

[1] " Dixit, eumque imis sub fluctibus audiit omnis
Nereidum Phorcique chorus, Panopeaque Virgo.
Et pater ipse manu magna Portunus euntem
Imputet."—*Aeneid.*

used to sound the tocsin to warn the bay of the approaching pirates.

Up there on yonder hill glisten the white houses of Massa Lubrense, crowned by orange and lemon-trees, and at the top of the mountain lies Deserto's gray old cloister.

Ah yes, the coast is beautiful indeed, but the bay is lovelier still, and blissfully we steer our course over the foaming billows!

You are sailing in Sorrento's bravest boat, not in such a one as the passing stranger hires at his hotel, 'tis only a simple fishing-boat, but if you are a connoisseur, you need only look at the graceful outline to assure yourself that it comes of good old stock. On board this boat you can go out fishing on the high seas, right out to Gaeta and the Bay of Terracina, the autumn hurricanes may even drive you over to Sicily—but that is of no consequence, this boat can weather any storm, for it was launched upon the

Blessed Virgin's birthday, and it can breast any wave, whilst the picture of its patron saint, San Antonio, hangs at the helm. See how the sharp keel cuts through the waves, just feel how quickly it responds to the lightest touch of your hand upon the rudder! It might almost be alive, you might almost be flying along upon some fiery war-horse with spark-emitting hoofs and foam-covered bridle.

That fellow sitting by the rudder is said to be a pessimist — well, well, if they all have that expression on their faces, the malady cannot be incurable. It is he who is convinced that in this world sorrow is positive and pleasure negative,—have you any idea what that means? Nay, no more have I. It is he who maintains that when man has resigned himself to his fate, he has attained the greatest heights to which he is capable of rising—no doubt it is resignation alone that shines in his eyes and plays about his lips. It is he who,

unknown to any one, has written a long
essay on the characteristics of melancholy,
which he declares are to be found exis-
tent in the features of all animals—look
out upon the dolphins as they sport in
front of our boat, have you ever seen
anything so melancholy as their turbulent
play upon the foaming waves! What
would Schopenhauer say if he could see
you both, if he could see thee, thou
pessimistic steersman, and you, ye sporting dolphins! Although there is something uncanny about these black and
brilliant dolphins—for just about here
where they are sporting at their best,
there stood, in bygone times, a temple
dedicated to Circe. Once upon a time,
long ago, I lay asleep upon the yellow
sands that surround the mermaids' castle,
and woke to the sound of the waves as
they began to sing the magic legends of
the old-time days, and as I opened my
eyes, I saw the graceful siren bathing
in the moonlight below, and far away

out in the bay, I heard the tritons blowing in their glittering conch-shells.

Now we pass the promontory of Campanella, and the wind blows high across Salerno's gulf.

Vincenzo was right—the sea is rough down there, and you had better come and sit by me and hold fast on to the tiller, whilst we have a chat together. Vincenzo is always right, he knows the sea by heart as surely as he knows his *Pater Noster*, and it is he who taught me how to steer a boat. He is satisfied with his pupil, and now is sitting forward, the weather-beaten old salt, with his clay pipe in his mouth, and the yellow cap of a Capriot fisherman well pulled down over his forehead, whilst his blinking eyes look critically across Salerno's bay, from whence the wind comes dancing over the breakers.

The youthful sailor sitting beside him is my friend Andrea. Do you know who Andrea is? Well, he is *il fratello della*

Marguerita, the beauty of Anacapri, whom all visitors to the island are as anxious to see as the villa of Tiberias or the Blue Grotto itself. She is now married to a *forestiero*, and I stood godfather to her first-born child last time I was here. Brother Andrea has been away as long as myself, four whole years, he has been round the world as sailor on board a French ship, and now he is on his way home to greet *la madre e la sorella*.

Our crew consists of forty men, and it would take up too much time to give you an account of each one of us, besides which, our story is more or less the same in every case. We are humble individuals every one of us, fishermen all, if you will, some of us have had good luck and others bad, there are shipwrecked souls amongst us too, there are those amongst us who have come to grief both over coral-fishing and medicine ; but the same joy is lighting up our eyes to-day, the joy of finding our-selves so near our lovely home once more.

We have been far away in foreign lands ;
we have seen other shores where we might
have lain us down to rest in peace, but
we have been faithful to our love, and
hither our longing thoughts have always
flown.   And now we have realised our
dreams, one hour more and we shall
haul in our sails upon our well-beloved
shores !

Hast thou seen the loveliest pearl in
Naples's crown, hast thou seen Isola di
Capri, floating upon the waters of the
bay ?   Its waves bathe richer shores than
thine, oh island fair, softer are the winds
that blow across Sorrento's groves, and
more bountifully o'er Ischia's hills than
o'er thy summer-laden rock has Nature
strewn her glory of green, but never doth
the sun shine with such dazzling splendour
as over Capri, never do the blue waters
of the bay sparkle so brilliantly as on thy
sun-girt shores !

The frivolous luxury of Naples's Queen
has not reached Capri.   The other vassals

round the bay have bowed the knee to the
fair sinner, who, according to the legend,
owes her name to some bewitching siren
of old, and who, as time went on, raised
temples to that Venus of whom Anacreon
and Ovid sang, whom marble has shaped
unto the likeness of the Venus Callipoge,
and who lives in the voluptuous beauty of
the Venus of the Capitol, and the Venus
of Medici.   But thou, severe and chaste,
untouched by degradation, thou standest
on thy sea-girt pedestal, even as the
Aphrodite of Melos, living the life of the
immortals, surrounded by the radiance
of the youth of Greece, and pure as
the ideal of Beauty itself!

Once did Rome violate thy virgin purity
with the shadow of her sun's departing
glory, but thou didst hurl the temple of
Tiberias into the sea, and there the coral-
incrusted columns lie unto this day, and
vines and honeysuckle grow over the
crumbling ruins that witnessed thy humili-
ation.

The poets have written verses in thine honour, and have compared thee to a dreaming sphinx or to an antique sarcophagus—I have no words for thee, thou soul-enchanting island, I am dumb before the charm of thy divine beauty! Ah! thoughts may clothe themselves in words, but believe me, the heart is silent, so silent that thou canst hear the wing-beating of thy soul. And here is my heart's own peaceful home; the noise of the outside world dies upon its threshold; and here in solitude would I reverently muse upon the faded memories of the past!

*   *

*

There are the white houses on the Marina shining brightly down upon us; and Francesco, standing at the prow, sings out that the beach is swarming with people.

And now Vincenzo produces from a

S

carefully wrapped-up parcel the present he has brought from afar, and which we are all called upon to look at and admire yet once again. The old fellow has had a hard time of it lately, so hard that he has been obliged to sell his Sunday clothes to buy his daily bread, and to-day is the first time he has had a smoke for ever so long—but the silk handkerchief that is to deck his wife when she shall go to Mass, that has never been touched. The old woman is to be depended upon, she has let many a big sea wash over her, as she has sat holding on to the tiller during the stormy autumn fishing nights ; and now she is sitting up at Anacapri, looking out over the bay, and mending the nets whilst she waits for the old man's return.

Nearly all the young fellows are coral fishermen, very likely they have each their "Nenella" waiting for them up yonder sighing for their return. And she shall have a coral necklace or a pretty pearl which he has put on one side on purpose for her. She has had many another offer of marriage in the meantime, the graceful maiden, and many an insinuating word has been whispered into her ear by various *Signori*, but her thoughts are with the absent one, and her word once given she will never swerve from it. No letters have passed between them during the long absence, for neither of them knows how to write, but every morning she has, for his sake, decked the Madonna's altar with fresh flowers, and as the storm rose high, and he was watching alone on deck, you may be sure he had a look at the blessed medal which she had hung around his neck the day they parted. She has an idea that he is close at hand, every day she has looked across the bay to see if he is coming, depend upon it she will be at the Marina when we lie-to. Has he been fortunate he will have saved up money enough to buy a boat, and that is quite enough to start upon if you love one another. And if he should never return

—coral-fishing is dangerous, and every year the ocean craves its victims—well, then she will hang the ring he has given her up in the choir, beside the altar.   Go up to yonder chapel and there you will find many and many a witness to this touching fidelity.

The beach really is swarming with people, and we can see many more running up the road that winds along the vineyards which grow in the neighbourhood of the Marina.   Close to the landing-stage stand the coastguards, the carabineers' guns are glittering in the sunshine.   They hang out the red flag, the first signal that bids us stop, and then they shout out something which we fail to catch, but which, alas, we are able to understand only too well—we haul in the sails and drop the anchor.   The guards are right, there is no doubt about it, I have read the quarantine rules myself, we have no right to come within twenty-five metres of the shore.

We anchored opposite the Marina during the whole of a never-to-be-forgotten day. I could write you many a long letter about that day and all we went through. But I keep my recollections of Capri to myself.

We never landed.

Silently I sat in the boat listening to my poor friends as they greeted their dear ones. More than one of our crew had been away for years and years, and it had been the thought of going home that had cheered them up through many a heavy hour, their own people stood now upon the beach, and they might not even take them to their arms! There were the old women shading their eyes with their hands, the better to distinguish the features of the returning son, there were the wives holding up the last-born *bambino* for his father to see how *carino* he had become, there were the young girls, decked in all their finery, to welcome home their sunburnt *amorosi*, all of them pressing up to the very edge of the harbour so as to approach as close as possible, eager little urchins threw themselves into the sea (do not be alarmed, they swim like fish, the little sunburnt devils), some of them laughing, some of them sobbing, all shouting together in the endeavour to be heard above the waves. And they managed to catch their word of welcome, each one of them. The lovely shore was the frame that surrounded the picture, and the sun of Italy shone full upon it.

And last of all, " *il Signore con lo cane* " ran up to the bow to greet all these good friends of his. He has lived so long amongst this people, and they all know him so well. See, there comes Serafina, hurrying up, " *buon giorno, cara Serafina!* " She had been his *serva* during the whole of one year, she had been so kind to him when he lay sick here, and he is so fond of her. For four years every morning has she dusted his old rooms,

she believes so firmly that he will return
again, and so does he in his happy
moments.

We lay anchored there all day long,
and all day long did Capri's kindly inhabitants stand on the shore waving us
their welcome and farewell. And the
evening crept on, the sun went down
behind Monte Epomeo, and the shadows
fell across the bay. Naples had lit up
her darkling festal halls, and over there
sat old Vesuvius calmly smoking his
evening pipe. The breeze grew softer
and ever more caressing, and the waves
fell asleep. Silently, as though in mourning, our boat sped over the bay, leaving
the well-loved shore behind us. Speechless we sat there, watching the gradual
disappearance of Capri into the darkness
beyond ; wafted by the wind the echo
of the dear voices on shore fell upon our
ears, and many of us saw the lights
twinkling in our own homes. A moment
more and all was still, and night fell over

the isle we loved so well, and spread her sable pall around her.

Ah yes! perhaps the poets are right, thou'rt like unto a sarcophagus! but leave the dead in peace, let silence shed its calm o'er thy departed joy! Here, beneath the roses and the evergreens, a youthful dream lies slumbering.

The wind has dropped, and the boat lies almost motionless upon the silent bay. But none of us are in a hurry to reach Sorrento; it will be time enough if we get there by to-morrow morning.

There sits Vincenzo holding his old wife's silken handkerchief in his hand, and if a spot should fall upon it, it shall become her all the more on that account, when at some future time she shall wear it in the church, for the weather-beaten old sailor is crying over it. And slowly Francesco stows away the corals which, this very evening, he had hoped to clasp round his Nenella's neck. But beside him sits Giovanni singing " Il Pescatore di Coralli "—

> " Addio, Lucia, m' appellano,
> Il vento già compare,
> Abbiam salpata l'ancora,
> La luna è in mezzo al mare,
> Mi sento il cor dividere,
> Partendomi da te !
> Speranza mia, non piangere
> Ch'è il marinar fedele
> Vedrai tornar dall' Africa
> Fra un anno queste vele.
> Ed all' ara della Vergine
> Allor sarai con me.
>   Addio, Addio,
>   Addio, Addio ! "

It is night upon the bay. And legend upon legend wakes the silent shores from their thousand-year-old dreams. The fair siren, to whom these regions were once dedicated, is casting her spell around thee.

Here lay the old Elysian fields, here lay Homer's kingdom of the dead ; 'twas here that Virgil's sybil led Æneas by the hand in search of his dead father, and 'twas past here that rolled the dark waves of the Cocytus.

Here did Augustus seek repose from his kingship over the world, here in Julius Cæsar's antique villa did Marcellus die, hither did Tiberias flee in search of the narcotic that was to numb the profoundest of all human sadness, here did Nero hatch his darkest plots, here is Agrippa's tomb. Here lay the country homes of Cicero and Lucullus, here did Ovid and Horace sing the beauties of the surrounding landscape, and here upon the shore he loved so well did Virgil cause his tomb to be hewn.[1]

The shadows of the night fall gradually away, and a faint light flutters over the gulf. But the shores lie slumbering still beneath the web the lingering stars and glittering moon have spun. Seest thou that little brilliant cloud rising over yonder mountain peak,—he is the herald of the day, and he it is who shall strew the

---

[1] " Mantuae me genuit, Calabri rapuere, tenet nunc Parthenope ; cecini pascua, rura, duces,"— epitaph written by the poet for his own tomb.

roses on the path by which the monarch
of the day shall drive.

And now the wind awakes, and scattering
the poppies from out Sorrento's curls, flies
upon the morning's roseate wings to Capri,
gently lifts the mist that shrouds the lovely
island, smooths away with fairy hand the
sleep that lays on Naples's eyes, and with
gentle breeze caresses Posilipo's blushing
cheek. Thus falls the veil of Night,
which hid the scenery around, even as the
draperies conceal the beauteous limbs of
an antique marble statue, and decked in
all the splendour of her divine apparel,
Naples salutes the rising sun. The bay
is clear as Diana's mirror, and the space
above so high that thou feelest as though
thou wert gazing into heaven itself.

And thou, thou poor, prosaic, everyday
individual, how humiliated dost thou not
feel at the spectacle of Nature's sublime
devotions, thou feelest that thou standest
upon the threshold of a temple and criest,
" *Here of a surety do the gods abide!* "

Yea, here do the gods abide indeed, and living still across the ages they pass before thee draped in Pentelic marble, the broken columns of the temples raise themselves on high soaring up to the heaven of eternal idealism, and it is not the dawn of a new day, ah no, it is the lingering glow of Antiquity's departed sun that sheds its lustre over the Golfo di Napoli.

XV

SŒUR PHILOMÈNE

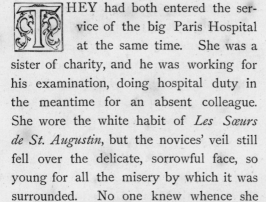THEY had both entered the service of the big Paris Hospital at the same time. She was a sister of charity, and he was working for his examination, doing hospital duty in the meantime for an absent colleague. She wore the white habit of *Les Sœurs de St. Augustin,* but the novices' veil still fell over the delicate, sorrowful face, so young for all the misery by which it was surrounded. No one knew whence she came, she was Sœur Philomène, that was all. Several of the young physicians in the *Salle de Garde* had done their best to find out who she was, but the only person capable perhaps of throwing any light

upon the subject was *La Supérieure*, and she observed a mysterious silence whenever the conversation turned upon the youthful sister of charity. It was always Sœur Philomène who, during the morning round was able to give on the patient's behalf the most trustworthy account of the previous night, it was always she who seemed to know better than any one else how to place the pillows most comfortably beneath the weary head of the poor sufferer, grown restless and fretful under the burden of his pain, it was always she who spoke the word of hope when the operation was at hand, and the courage on the wane. And when the night-bell rang into the Salle de Garde below, and he who was on duty came up, tired and irritable, to see what was wanted of him, it was she again who always led the way, bending gently over the patient's bed, laying the bandages straight with her own soft hands and soothing the agony of the night with words of comfort and good cheer.

One night a boy who had been found lying senseless in the street was brought in from a neighbouring police station. He was bleeding from a wound in the head, and was perfectly stiff with cold. After the first bandages had been adjusted, Sœur Philomène undressed him quickly, and laid him in a warmed bed. He was a poor man's child, and a suit of tattered old clothes was all that sheltered his frail little body from the severity of the winter's night. For some time he lay there quite unconscious, but then he began to moan softly, raising his hand to his head. After a while he opened his eyes, the large wistful eyes of early childhood, gazing at the white curtains about his bed, and then across the dimly-lighted sickroom. Presently, the little half-thawed fingers began to wander over the counterpane, both hands groping restlessly about the bed as though in search of something ; he looked quieter after he had managed to possess himself of the tiny old fiddle which he always carried about with him under his jacket, and which constituted the whole of his luggage.

Grasping it tightly he suddenly raised himself up as though to escape. The poor homeless little lad, accustomed as he was to being turned away from every man's door, was under the impression that danger was ahead, and having recovered his fiddle, the returning dawn of consciousness warned him that he had better be off. But his head was too heavy, and he soon fell back again amongst the pillows. Just then he became aware of the fact that a man was standing at the head of his bed, and with wide open, suspicious eyes he stared at his blood-stained apron. The doctor saw that he was frightened and moved away. But as Sœur Philomène bent over the little fellow at the same moment he grew calmer, looking her straight in the face somewhat curiously, but with an expression of unbounded confidence in his eyes.

And the doctor went and laid himself

down in the watch-room. He was just at
that period of a young physician's life,
when it is considered rather a fine thing
to show no compassion for the sick, to
affect an imperturbable self-possession on
all occasions, when down in the Salle de
Garde each one tries to outdo the other
in cold-blooded assurances of his own
complete indifference to all suffering, when
the patient is merely a number attached
to the living and breathing designs which
the hospital draws into their pathological
book of references, and the corpse is
nothing better than a *cadaver* to be examined critically from an anatomical point
of view alone. . . .

And as he lay there in the watch-room,
he thought that he was quite indifferent
to the poor little waif up in the Salle St.
Paul.

But he could not go to sleep, and after
tossing about for while, he persuaded himself that perhaps it would be as well to go
and see whether the bandages round the

T

boy's head were still in order, and whether
the hemorrhage had definitively ceased.
On the stairs he stopped short, saying to
himself that there was really nothing more
for him to do upstairs that night, and that
the boy had much better be left in peace.
But somehow or other he went up.   They
had been round for the last time that night,
and the room was quite quiet.   He crept
stealthily up to the newcomer's bed.
Sœur Philomène was sitting there still,
the homeless little musician had fallen
asleep with one arm round the sister of
charity's neck, and his fiddle in the other
hand.

And during the next morning's round
he was to be enlightened as to the reason
why he, the callous young medical student,
had been unable to resist the impulse that
had led him to go and look after the boy
the previous night.   No one knew where
the lad came from, to all the questions put
to him he was silent, for all answer staring
at the little group of students and pro-

fessors that had gathered round his bed. But just as a speculative assistant began to write the following words upon the slate hanging over his bed, "*Commotion cérébrale, perte de la parole,*" the boy put his little thumb into his mouth, blinked his eyes and smacked his lips, to the utter astonishment of every one present. And there was one standing by his bedside who understood him, — Mergellina and Santa Lucia had familiarised him long ago with that same sign. "*Tu sei Italiano?*" he asked him.

"*Si Signore, vengo da Napoli,*" answered the little lazzarone. He was not in the least dumb, only frightened of all the strange people and their foreign language.

But the little lad had secured a good friend for himself, and one who was only too glad to look after him.

The boy's story was the usual one. He came from one of the poor mountain villages round Salerno, and had been accustomed to wander through the streets of

Naples with his fiddle under his arm to earn his bread. Thence he had been brought to Paris as a speculation. Every year these white slave-traders come over to Naples, selecting their victims amongst its swarms of ragged street-children, taking them back to London or Paris, where they are then expected to earn a little money as street-singers or models.

The child is presented with new clothes, and the parents (if there be any) are easily pacified by means of a small sum of money, and the promise that the boy shall return in a year's time with a 100 lire in his pocket. Such is the history of most of the Italian children who wander about the streets of Paris. The money they earn they are not allowed to keep ; every night their *impresario* takes away from them whatever they have scraped together during the day.

The boy had not been in Paris for more than a few days, but he had lost his way, and had wandered aimlessly about till, exhausted with cold and hunger, he had fainted in the street.

But the winter's night had been more than the destitute little Southerner had been able to bear. As the day wore on he began to cough, towards night-time he was in a high fever. Next morning the slate over his bed bore the following inscription "*Pneumonie double*"—and this time, alas, the diagnosis was correct enough.

For three nights Sœur Philomène watched over the poor little musician, and on the fourth day he died.

No one had taken the least notice of him before, he had belonged to no one during his lifetime, but after his death he belonged by right to the dissecting-room. He was hardly cold before one of the hospital servants came to fetch away the frail little body, to take it down to be cut to pieces by the dissecting-knives of the students. Sœur Philomène and the doctor were still standing beside the bed, and involuntarily they glanced at each

other. And he who had been so power-
less to save the life of his little friend now
drew the sheet over his face, and beckoned
silently to the man to delay his errand;
and then he went down to *Monsieur le
directeur*. He was in the good graces of
the hospital authorities just then, and they
granted his request.

And towards the close of day a tiny
coffin was borne from out the hospital
walls; there was no long funeral proces-
sion; a sister of charity and a student
alone walked behind the hearse, wherein
the poor little vagabond artist lay at rest
with his broken fiddle in his hands. And
of all those flowers, which in midwinter
the luxury of the world's great capital
imports every morning from the summer
of the south, a handful of violets had
found its way into the curly-headed little
musician's coffin, bearing a fragrant greeting from the land of his birth, where,
perhaps, that very night, up in the little
mountain-chapel, his poor mother was

praying her heart out to the Blessed Virgin, beseeching her to watch over her darling cast adrift on the world.

* *

*

Sœur Philomène was just as silent now as she had always been, she never spoke to any one, unless it were to ask some short question imposed upon her by the exigencies of hospital duty. But they seemed to have something in common, these two friends of the little dead child. Had she some special *protégé* in her ward, he always managed to look after him himself, and did he happen to be particularly interested in some patient or other, it seemed to him as though the gentle sister always contrived to show them some special attention.

There were twelve sisters of charity up at the big hospital. *La Supérieure,* "*ma mère,*" as they all called her, had done her little best to convert the foreign assistant,

for she knew that he was not of the same
faith as themselves, the faith that had bid
her sacrifice her life beneath the veil of a
sister of charity; one day she asked him
if they never went to confession in his
church, if they never lit candles upon the
Blessed Virgin's altar, and as he answered in the negative, the old nun had
shaken her head compassionately but re-
signedly.

But they were none the less friendly on
that account; he had even been allowed
to play during "*La Grande Messe*" on the
tiny organ in the little chapel, one day
that the old brother, who usually officiated
as organist, was ill.

And by way of thanks he tried, as far
as lay in his power, to plead the cause of
the sisters of charity in the daily discussions that took place down in the Salle de
Garde. The unjust and shameful persecu-
tion directed against them, *la laïcisation
des hopitaux*, was the burning question of
the day, and all their unselfishness, all

their self-sacrificing charity had not availed to silence the voices of those whose sole object was to exclude religious influence of every sort from the hospitals.

Every evening prayers were read down in the little chapel for the benefit of those who were able to attend, after which each sister read the prayers for the night in her own special ward. Often and often after supper the young doctor would linger for a few moments up in the Salle St. Paul. As Sœur Philomène lit the candles on the little altar, the moaning and groaning would gradually cease, and a hush would fall over the whole room; kneeling in the midst of them the sister's pure voice would be heard praying that rest might be vouchsafed during the coming night, concluding with the *Ave Maria*, which all the sick repeated after her. Some of them were not always able to follow her, and every now and again some tired voice would lag behind the others with the finishing words : " *Priez pour nous, pauvres pêcheurs, maintenant et à l'heure de notre mort!* "   And from some of the beds nothing would be heard but a faint inarticulate murmur—but it found its way along with the rest for all that.

Sœur Philomène was looking very pale.   One day she was missing from the usual morning round, and it was reported that she had spat blood during the night. But she was soon at her post again, as devoted as ever ; night and day she was to be found in the wards, succouring and comforting the sick, and never pausing to give herself a moment's rest.

And so the winter sped away.   The windows stood open all day long, and the soft spring breezes penetrated at last into the dreary wards, floating from bed to bed, lifting up the curtains behind which the pallid sufferers lay, waiting upon their last resource—the summer.

The trees were beginning to put forth their leaves in the garden beneath, and out on the terrace the convalescents would sit for hours together, warming themselves in the sun.

They were making merry down in the Salle de Garde, and every one was toasting the newly-made doctor for the last time. There on the wall hung his old hospital uniform, covered with stains and saturated with carbolic acid, and there, amidst books and commentaries, lay the old pipe that had kept him company during many a hard night's work. There he sat in travelling dress, the long-desired diploma in his pocket, and up in his old room lay his knapsack all ready packed for the morrow's journey. Every one was talking, and no one was listening. At last the doctor manages to escape, wending his way once more up to the well-known passage leading to the Salle St. Paul. He stood in the doorway and heard the whisper pass from bed to bed, "*la ronde de la mère!*" And there, holding the night-lamp in her hand, came

Sœur Philomène from the other end of
the half-dark dormitory.   He looked at
the sorrowful pallid face, and realised how
much he had learnt to care for the meek
and gentle sister, although he had hardly
ever spoken a word to her.   After she had
finished her round, he went up to bid her
farewell.   He was going far away, and
perhaps he might never see her again, but
before leaving, he felt that he must say
how much it grieved him to see *la bonne
Sœur* looking so pale, so ill, and then he
told her to think a little of herself, that
she was killing herself with her incessant
devotion to the sick.   " I am happy," was
all she answered.   He forgot the severe
convent rules to which her vows had
bound her, and stretched out his hand to
bid her farewell,—but she did not take it.

He was gone for a long, long time.   One
evening he stood again in front of the old
hospital.   It looked just the same as ever,
the dingy walls were harbouring the same
amount of suffering and woe as in the

days of old. It was just about the time when Sœur Philomène used to read the evening prayers up in the Salle St. Paul, and he thought he would go up there. But the little altar had been knocked down, the crucifix was nowhere to be seen, la Sœur Philomène was gone, all the friendly sisters had disappeared. A student clad in the well-known hospital uniform was coming towards him,—perhaps he would be able to tell him all he wanted to know.

"*Ah, oui, les Sœurs! il y'a longtemps qu'on les a mises à la porte!*"

"Just so, my young friend, *il y'a longtemps qu'on les a mises à la porte.*"

"And the white-haired old chaplain of the hospital, is he here still?"

"*Il n'y a plus de prêtres ici, il n'y a plus d'église, à quoi bon!*"

"But you must have been here before," asked the student, eyeing the foreign visitor with some curiosity. "It must have been before my time?"

"Yes, it must have been before your time."

It must have been long, long ago, thought he to himself as he turned to go, for he felt so out of date and out of place in the tide of all these modern improvements. He lingered about the garden for a while, watching the light shine through the window of his former room. Very likely a new student was sitting there, reading for his examination——may he go further into the history of suffering humanity than his predecessor standing in the garden below, for he never got further than the chapter on man's utter helplessness, and there he marked the book with a cross.

*   *

*

It was several years later. The doctor had taken leave of his Paris duties for a while, and was again on his way to greet the land he loved so well. He was not

altogether idle, for idleness begets hypochondria. However, he didn't study much
either—after all he was taking his holiday.
Every one else was writing long treatises
on the cholera—but he didn't write a line
on the subject, for the simple reason that
he had nothing to say. And the microbes,
the celebrated microbes, which, small as
they are, have nevertheless been the means
of making many a doctor great—he did
not trouble himself about them either.
He felt about as much inclination to gaze
at one of them through a microscope, as
to examine the far away glittering stars
of Heaven by means of a telescope—what
he saw with his own eyes was enough for
him. And he saw with sorrow how much
the poor people were suffering.

The cholera decreased, but the famine
in the land grew worse and worse. He
did not often go up to the hospital ; those
who were lying there stood in no need of
his assistance ; better doctors than himself
were giving their services, and charity was

being freely bestowed upon the families of the sick. One evening, however, he went up to the cholera hospital, for he had been told that a French sister of charity was lying there on the point of death.

In the corridor he met an assistant with whom he was slightly acquainted. In answer to his question he pointed to the door of one of the reserved rooms, " *stadium algidum*," [1] said he, and went on his way.

The room was half dark, two sisters of charity were kneeling within, and on the bed lay Sœur Philomène, as pale as death. Slowly she opened her eyes, and her glance fell straight on him who stood sorrowing at her bedside.

" I knew you were here," she said. And then she reached him her hand—but it was hers no more, it no longer belonged to life, it was already quite cold. Presently she fell asleep again, lying there

---

[1] A characteristic of the cholera when the body is cold.

quite motionless, opening her eyes every now and again to gaze fixedly and at length at those who stood about her bed. Towards morning she began to shiver, and they drew the folds of her nun's white garb still closer round her. She was already quite cold, but one could see by her eyes that she was in full possession of her senses. Her lips moved as though she wished to say something, but all power of speech had fled. The painful shadow over the forehead, which he recognised so well, vanished little by little as her eyes began to glow with a joy of which this world knows nothing. And then her soul took wing, and the peace of death fell over her face.

And those who stood around — they knew that she was happy.

Printed by R. & R. CLARK, *Edinburgh.*

U